Learn to Pray

Biblical Doctrine of Prayer

Martin Murphy

Learn to Pray

Published by: Theocentric Publishing Group
               1069A Main Street
               Chipley, FL 32428

               http://www.theocentricpublishing.com

Library of Congress Control Number: 2016903998

ISBN 9780986405563

To my mother, Kate Hopper Murphy, who prayed for me before I was old enough to pray.

Foreword

I am impressed with this book on the subject of *Learn to Pray*. It is stated briefly and succinctly following the model and example of the Lord's Prayer. There is considerable practical instruction on the meaning and implication about purposeful and biblical prayer and it will serve as a useful primer for all who apply the prayer principles. The reader will doubtlessly return to the instruction frequently for the practical help it offers. Although there are many fanciful ideas and miscalculations regarding prayer, this brief volume dissects several of them and clears the pathway of debris so the reader can gain the benefit from prayer that pleases God.

What is the correct motivation and perspective for prayer? Generally, are the prayers expressed more inward or upward? A person recently wrote on Facebook: "Why do you pray? I pray because I am desperate for God to hear me. Why? Because 'my soul is full of troubles' and I have no strength of my own. I need God's ear, his face, his help. Prayer, in part, is a desperate cry to God. It is also an expectant heave sent to heaven. Early each morning, I cry to God. (Psalm 88)." The use of Psalm 88 Is a reflection of how overwhelmed one can be and the darkness that floods the soul of the one given to human introspection apart from the spiritual balance through one's relationship to God in Christ.

One Church's Creedal Statement asks the question, "What Is Prayer?" The answer given is: "Prayer is an offering up of our desires unto God, for things agreeable to his will, in the name of Christ,‒with confession of our sins, and thankful acknowledgment of his mercies." The volume, *Learn to Pray*, expands on this definition and is designed to be a practical encouragement as it guides one into an objective motivation in prayer. Even though the word "Doctrine" appears on the front cover, it is not a theological treatise on the subject of prayer. It uses The Lord's Prayer as the model and example for the proper approach as and when one prays. This Prayer is not supposed to be viewed as a "ritual" or a required part of one's worship experience. The purpose of the example and model for prayer has a much different design and purpose. There was a chorus often sung in Sunday Schools that contained the words: "Jesus and Others and You, what a wonderful way to spell J. O. Y." That idea also resonates in this important guideline as we *Learn to Pray*. Prayer entails one's focus on the Godhead with reverence and awe. The Prayer also entails the necessary actions and interactions of life in terms of dependence upon God and the acknowledgement of human frailties. One needs God's faithful supply, but much more His forgiveness and guidance through the pathway of life. Biblical prayer should conclude with a resounding benediction regarding the Lord's kingdom, power and glory.

The Lord's Prayer can be understood as a focus upon worship of the triune God, especially with the words: "Our Father, who resides in Heaven!" and "Hallowed be Your name!" Too often prayer is viewed tritely and in a matter-of-fact manner. There must be the understanding and sense that one is coming before and being in the presence of almighty God. As one ponders prayer and how to approach God, there are a couple of important encouragements for the biblical Christian. In Isaiah 65:24 (NKJV), "And it shall come to pass, that before they call, I will answer; and while they are yet speaking, I will hear." God is anticipating one's coming to Him with requests and His response is already determined. He is ready and willing to respond to His people when they come to Him for His help in their time of need. This needs to be coupled with Romans 8:26-27 (ESV), "Likewise the Spirit helps us in our weakness. For we do not know what to pray for as we ought, but the Spirit himself intercedes for us with groaning too deep for words. And he who searches hearts knows what is the mind of the Spirit, because the Spirit intercedes for the saints according to the will of God." Additionally, we also have the words of Paul who wrote about this moment in worship and prayer in Ephesians 3:20 (NIV), "Now to him who is able to do immeasurably more than all we ask or imagine, according to his power that is at work within us." This volume will assist in guiding the reader to know the fullness that results from one's loving the presence of God and the times of coming before God. The reminder in I Thessalonians 5:16-18 to: "Rejoice always, pray without ceasing, give thanks in all circumstances; for this is the will of God in Christ Jesus for you!" serves as a reminder for the conscious reality of what it means to walk and live in the presence of God always. Prayer can be offered to God at any time, in any place and in any circumstance. Posture in prayer and location for prayer is not a determinative factor that limits one's valid expressions to God in whose presence one lives and moves and has one's being.

The words of the model Prayer should be underscored and indelibly traced upon one's heart and mind, as well as being etched in one's soul. The focus of worshipful prayer is: Thy name be Hallowed; Thy Kingdom come; Thy Will be done. Prayer is not one telling God a story or making demands of what is wanted. When applying a passage such as Philippians 4:6 (NIV), "Do not be anxious about anything, but in every situation, by prayer and petition, with thanksgiving, present your requests to God..." one must be very careful to follow the requisites established by Jesus Christ in the model prayer.

The author points out the sincerity that is required in terms of personal confession and forgiveness. The practice of one praying is vital in terms of the prayer God will hear and answer. If one is approaching God in prayer with his own personal interpretations of it, the Scriptural counsel echoed in James 1:7-8 would be applicable where James wrote that the double-minded man should have no expectation of receiving anything from the Lord. As a matter of fact, the author correctly states in Chapter 5 that "The Lord's model prayer is a prayer for professing Christians only..." If one refuses to be convicted and convinced by the Holy Spirit (John 16:7-11) of sin, righteousness and judgment, such a one is under the judgment and condemnation of God. If one refuses to acknowledge Jesus Christ as Savior, Lord and Master, there is no one that can serve as the advocate and intercessor before the Father in heaven (I Timothy 2:4-6). The author rightly points out in Chapter 6 the usage of the words debts and trespasses. He summarizes that we would do well to relate those words to the sin reality with which one must deal.

In conjunction with that summation, Ephesians 2:1 (NKJV) records this statement: "And you He has made alive who were dead in trespasses and sins." *The Berean Publication* posts: "Trespasses, from the Greek *paraptoma,* means "to go off a path, fall or slip aside." When it is applied to moral and ethical issues it means to deviate from the right way, to wander. Sins, the Greek *hamartia,* is generally associated with military usage and means to "miss the mark." It indicates failing to make a bull's-eye. In moral and ethical contexts, it means to fail of one's purpose, to go wrong, or to fail to live according to an accepted standard or ideal. Sin is the failure to be what we ought to be and could be."

There is an assumption that is indicated in Chapter 8 and the important need to pray for one another. Jesus makes the assumption as well in the terms He employs regarding His followers with the usage of "when" and "as" one prays. It is set forth as being the normal practice of the biblical Christian. Jesus is stating the obvious that just as breathing is necessary for life in the physical body, prayer is even a more essential necessity within the spiritual body. In Chapter 12, there is a comprehensive appeal in the Prayer for Christian Living. The reference is Colossians 1:15-20 (NIV) which is significant because of the strong declaration of the deity of Jesus Christ and the oneness of the triune God in the latter part of the context:

> For in him all things were created: things in heaven and on earth, visible and invisible, whether thrones or powers or rulers or authorities; all things have been created through him and for him. He is before all things, and in him all things hold together. And he is the head of the body, the church; he is the beginning and the firstborn from among the dead, so that in everything he might have the supremacy. For God was pleased to have all his fullness dwell in him, and through him to reconcile to himself all things, whether things on earth or things in heaven, by making peace through his blood, shed on the cross. (Colossians 1:15-20)

The thrust for one who is praying to the One who created and sustains all things is a tacit understanding that the One, Jesus Christ, is more than sufficient in the concern He has for the detail of one's life.

When the disciples asked Jesus Christ to teach them to pray (Luke 11), it echoes into each of our lives where the vacuum and void within the soul can and should be filled with the guidelines and biblical instruction on the need and possibilities of prayer. May the Lord bless and enrich your life as you gain a greater understanding of meaningful and biblical prayer.

A Hymn that can be used as a prayer expression was written and composed by Albert Simpson Reitz (1879-1966):

> Teach me to pray, Lord, teach me to pray;
> This is my heart-cry day unto day;
> I long to know Thy will and Thy way;
> Teach me to pray, Lord, teach me to pray.

Power in prayer, Lord, power in prayer!
Here 'mid earth's sin and sorrow and care,
Men lost and dying, souls in despair;
O give me power, power in prayer!

JAMES PERRY

Table of Contents

Table of Contents

1. Pray to Our Heavenly Father

Our Father in heaven...

Luke 11:1-4

The model prayer recorded in the Gospel of Luke was given at the request of a disciple (Luke 11:1-4). "Lord teach us to pray" (Luke 11:1). The word "teach" in the Greek text is in the imperative mood, which means the disciple commanded Jesus. Although it is properly an injunction, in the context it is an appeal, the strongest form of an appeal to the second person of the Trinity. The Gospel of Matthew has similar instruction from the Lord Jesus Christ (Matthew 6:5-13). The Luke version is essentially the same, but it is abridged and the minor differences in the prayer obviously teach us that Christ did not intend for them to be repeated word for word, because they serve only as a model.

The text in Matthew states two general principles in the negative. "And when you pray, do not use vain repetitions as the heathen do for they think that they will be heard for their many words" (Matthew 6:7). The first negative principle is "do not use vain repetitions." Vain repetition refers to worthless words. They are babbling words or could be translated "strange tongues." Excessive pompous religious words do not necessarily reveal a heart and passion for God. The second negative principle is do not "use many words." Copious words do not necessarily reflect a right relationship with God. They may use many false words, but God only wants truthful words. "The Lord is near to all who call upon Him, to all who call upon Him in truth" (Psalm 145:18).

The first half of the Lord's model prayer is about the nature and character of God. The second half of the Lord's model prayer is about the relationship of God to His people. It begins with an invocation of regalia. "Our Father in heaven" reveals the tenderness of God's presence among His people, but at the same time it reveals the transcendence of God. "Our Father" brings all Christians on the same playing field. It is not "My Father" as if it was a private individual affair, but "our Father" which is a collective term for the whole church. This model prayer is for believers only, thus "our Father." Praying "our Father" is utter nonsense and blasphemy for any who have not by grace through faith rested on and received Jesus Christ for eternal salvation.

The people who pray according to this model prayer have the same thing in common: "Our Father." God's people have an inseparable relationship; therefore, prayer, like every Christian doctrine, must demonstrate unquestionable integrity. I've heard people say, "I can't discuss religion with my neighbor." Both of them claim to be Protestants, but they are in different denominations. Both of them say they believe what is commonly referred to as "The Lord's Prayer." If they can't discuss their religious views with one another, then they are liars to say "Our Father." They would have to change the word "our" to "my" Father. I have read some books that focus on "how to pray" and some of them suggest changing this part of the model prayer to "my Father." They shift from the biblical model and doctrine to the therapeutic relationship model.

The first and most nagging problem with the lack of unity began in the Garden of Eden. The Bible expresses this problem in these terms: "I am and there is no one else besides me" (Isaiah 47:10). That attitude resides in the deepest crevice of the human soul. It changes the entire makeup of man's soul. It is no longer "Our Father in Heaven." It is "My Father in Heaven." It is the deep dark sin that prevents the collective church from saying "Our Father" with a sense of integrity.

Jesus instructed the disciples in the manner that demands agreement on understanding who the Father is. "When you pray say: Our Father in Heaven...." Therefore, Christians must understand who the "Father" is based on the teaching from the full counsel of God. Before I explain a few of the attributes of God the Father, remember the principles already established by Jesus Christ. Prayer should not include babbling words, no long prayer just to sound pompous and pious. Most importantly pray according to the truth of Scripture.

Although prayer does not necessarily require direct discourse to God about His characteristics, prayer offered to God must assume an understanding of God's nature and character. There are essentials that the collective church must have and agree with to say "Our Father."

The Bible explains that "God is Spirit" (John 4:24). The spirituality of God, often dismissed by professing Christians, should be at the forefront of any prayer. Christians learn and must believe the Spirit dimension from the Bible. It does not need to be a fairy tale kind of belief. It may be deduced that from a material creation there is a spiritual dimension.

The self-existence of God is another aspect of God's character to be considered when Christians pray to Him. God is independent. God cannot be the cause of Himself, thus making God independent in all His perfections. This leaves the person in prayer totally dependent upon the independent Father.

Praying to our Father in Heaven requires an abundance of faith. Christians have to believe that God is sufficient in all His perfections meaning that God is infinite. "But will God indeed dwell on the earth? Behold, heaven and the heaven of heavens cannot contain You" (1 Kings 8:27). Our Father in heaven has no limits or bounds, either actual or potential according to His nature.

I have heard people say something like this: "Sometime I wonder if my prayers are not bouncing off the ceiling." They are the people that need to understand God's nature and character. The Psalmist explained the eternal nature of God in graphic terms.

> Of old You laid the foundation of the earth, and the heavens are the work of Your hands. They will perish, but You will endure; Yes, they will all grow old like a garment: Like a cloak You will change them, and they will be changed. But You are the same, and Your years will have no end. (Psalm 102:25-27)

In a world of constant changes, the nature and character of God never changes. Christians pray to God with confidence in the immutable Father (James 1:17). Since God never changes, His goodness reveals the immensity of His love. Understanding who God is and what God does should cause every Christian to pray "our Father."

There are three words, known as three of the cardinal doctrines of the Christian religion, that without them, prayer is nonsense. They are omnipresence, omniscience, and omnipotence. Omnipresence refers to God's presence everywhere at once (Psalm 139:7-8). It is important because it means that prayer may be spoken to God anywhere, day or night or anytime. God's omniscience refers to God's knowledge (Proverbs 15:3; Acts 15:18). To put it another way, God knows everything past, present, and future. Omnipotence describes the all-powerful nature of God.

Prayer must be offered to "our Father in heaven" with full knowledge of His nature and character. The brief commentary published in the *Doctrine of Sound Words: Summary of Christian Theology* summarizes the preface to the Lord's model prayer.

> This prayer is only for believers who have a personal relationship with their heavenly Father through the Lord Jesus Christ. The Apostle Paul

reminds Christians they, "are all sons of God through faith in Christ Jesus" (Galatians 3:34). This model prayer is utter nonsense and blasphemy for any who are without the grace of God. However, the Lord's model prayer is most sensible for those children who have a Father in heaven.

This prayer may be difficult for those who do not have a good understanding of "fatherly goodness." If you had never heard sound biblical teaching about God the Father, the word "father" would and probably still does in some sense, bring to your mind an image of your earthly father. Christians must put aside all those thoughts and start over with a new understanding of their heavenly "Father." The natural earthly father may have been abusive and demonstrated his unkindness in spiteful and caustic ways. Our Father in heaven is totally different from our earthly father.

Our Father in heaven is sovereign, dignified above all other personalities, and demonstrates the most excellent divine perfections that can be imagined. Our Father in heaven is our Creator, our owner and benefactor in whom we live and move and have our being. The *Westminster Shorter Catechism* describes our Father in heaven as Spirit, infinite, eternal and unchangeable in his being, wisdom, power, holiness, justice, goodness, and truth. Our Father in heaven has dignity and honor above our understanding because of His transcendent nature, yet He has made a gracious condescension for the sake of His elect. He is a Father who is very near, yet He waits in heaven for you to pray to him saying, "Our Father in heaven." (*Doctrine of Sound Words: Summary of Christian Theology*, by Martin Murphy, p. 405-406)

The human race may choose which father they will serve

and therefore, which one they will worship in prayer. Christians will choose God the Father because they know Him and all His attributes based on the full counsel of God. Unbelievers will choose Satan the liar and deceiver. Christians may take pleasure in appearing before their Father in heaven.

The Doctrine of prayer requires a Mediator. The Lord Jesus Christ is the only acceptable Mediator.

The Lord Jesus Christ commands us to pray in His name, but the context and the purpose of the command is often ignored. Jesus said He will do whatever is asked in His name (John 14:13). Christians often take this as their carte blanche for any whimsical request from God. The reason Jesus does whatever is asked is so that "the Father may be glorified in the Son" (John 14:13).

A prayer is a frivolous prayer if the name of Jesus Christ is mentioned for selfish purposes. In His commentary on John 16:24, Dr. William Hendriksen's exposition is, "the mere mentioning of the name [Jesus Christ] would [not] help any. Certainly, when a believer concludes his prayer by saying, 'All this we ask in Jesus' name,' he is not using a magic formula. What he means is, "We ask all this on the basis of Christ's merits and in harmony with his redemptive revelation."

Christian prayers are rightfully presented to God in the name of Christ who alone is "the mediator between God and man" (1 Timothy 2:5). When "God's dread majesty come to mind" says John Calvin, "we cannot but tremble and be driven far away by the recognition of our own unworthiness, until Christ comes forward as intermediary, to the throne of dreadful glory into the throne of grace" (*Institutes of the Christian Religion,* 3.20.17). It would not be possible to approach God with confidence unless Christ "stands" on our behalf. Since man is a sinner and God cannot tolerate sin, it is by necessity that we draw our encouragement to pray from Christ. Christians have every reason to hope in the acceptance of their prayers when it is offered in the name of Christ who gives them boldness and strength. (*Doctrine of Sound Words*, by Martin Murphy, p. 400)

2. Pray to Dignify the Name of God

Hallowed be Your name...

Luke 11:1-4

Jesus taught His disciples to pray by bringing the whole counsel of God in perspective. Jesus used an occasion recorded in Matthew 6:9-13 and in Luke 11:1-4 to teach His disciples the manner of prayer. The text in Matthew and Luke are commonly called the "Lord's Prayer." However, Jesus was so intimately associated with every word in the Bible, He gave His disciples the basic principles necessary to engage in prayer according to the Word of God. The model prayer begins with the invocation, "our Father in Heaven." The prayer acknowledges the collective joining together of the church to worship in prayer and bringing petitions before "our Father in Heaven."

The first petition in this model prayer is to hallow the name of God. The biblical text "Hallowed be thy name" (Luke 11:2) literally means to give God's name the highest place of respect, honor, dignity and majesty. A brief glimpse of how the word "hallow" was derived from the Old and New Testament will help you understand the biblical meaning of the petition "Hallowed be thy name." The Latin word *consecratio* is translated to the English word "consecration" that is also translated "hallow." The Greek word *hagiazo* used in Matthew and Luke translates to English as "hallow" and in John's Gospel it translates to the English as "sanctify" (John17:19). Hallow is also derived from the Hebrew word *qadash* which literally means to "make holy" or "set apart." The force of the word "hallow" in English is found in the ancient biblical languages under one general heading: to make sacred or to make holy. Something is hallowed by consecrating it, sanctifying it or setting it apart as holy.

Prayer should begin with these words embedded on your soul's mind: "Lord, hallowed be your name." You may say those words with your mouth, but you must know what they mean based on the teaching of the whole Bible. Before Christians pray they ought to understand what it means to hallow the name of God.

The name of God originated in Semitic languages recorded in the Hebrew text in what is known today as the Old Testament. God's name necessarily describes how He has revealed himself in creation, in providence and especially in His redemptive power. Names used in the Old Testament often revealed something about that person. The Old Testament uses dozens of words to describe God. The Hebrew word *el* was a universal name for God and the gods of other Ancient Near Eastern religions. It referred to God's power and authority. Another word used in the Hebrew text in reference to the Lord (God of Israel) is a *Tetragrammaton*. This is a technical word that deserves more explanation.

> The four consonants YHWH forming the Hebrew incommunicable name of the Supreme Being that is translated "I AM WHO I AM." The Israelites replaced the word *Yahweh* with *Adonai* (both names translate to English as Lord) because they believed Yahweh was too sacred and therefore unapproachable with a common word. (*Theological Terms in Layman Language*, by Martin Murphy, p. 101)

There are many names for God that are more adjectival in their translation. A few of His names: Father, Judge, Redeemer, Savior, Deliverer, Rock, Shield, Strength, Righteous One, et al. Not understanding God's names deprives prayer of its proper place in private, family, or collective worship. Prayer is a feature of the soul that is ever in the presence of God. For that reason know, "The LORD of hosts, Him you shall hallow..." (Isaiah 8:13).

When Christians hallow (set God apart as holy) the name of the true and living God, it is necessary to grasp his identity, because his identity reveals His nature and character. His name impresses upon His people the reality of His imminence and transcendence. Christian prayer presupposes these thoughts of God.

> For behold, He who forms mountains, and creates the wind, who declares to man what his thought is, and makes the morning darkness, who treads the high places of the earth— The Lord God of hosts is His name. (Amos 4:13)

God's redeemed people have the privilege to pray to the hallowed One. "As for our Redeemer, the LORD of hosts is His name, The Holy One of Israel" (Isaiah 47:4). To hallow the name of God is to give Him the highest place of honor, dignity, and majesty. When Christians bow humbly and reverently to hallow God's name, they must remember God created them from dirt. His name must be set apart from all abuses and lift up His name above all names.

Christians can hallow God's name by offering holy and spiritual worship. Prayer should not be separated from spiritual worship. It is a holy devotion that comes from the heart of a converted sinner. The greatness of God ought to be evident by the humility of the sinner. One of the reasons young people are leaving the church as a religious organization is because they do not sense the transcendence of God in worship. The sense of the supernatural has been obscured by "churches smelling of coffee and reverberating with edgy music...put together in a package to please, entice, entertain, relax, grab and enfold potential customers, and worm its way into their hearts" (*The Courage to Be Protestant*, by David Wells, p. 14). When the church acts like a civic club, the best civic club wins. Church x has the best programs with the big and fancy building, and the sweetest preacher and he wears store bought torn blue jeans during worship. Unfortunately, they ignore the spirituality of the soul and the supernatural nature of God.

Christians hallow God's name by feeling grief and pain if God's name is dishonored. Praying to God using frivolous references to His name is profanity because God's name must be set apart as holy. God's name is dishonored by co-mingling truth with error.

Offering prayer to God without setting His name apart as holy is useless to the person offering prayer and detestable to God who hears the prayer. The best way to hallow God's name is to gather a sound knowledge of God. It is found in the Word of God. Let His name and His attributes live in your inner most being. Understanding God's name, will lead you to understand who God is which will lead to "pray without ceasing" to your Father in heaven.

3. Pray for God's Kingdom to Come

Your kingdom Come...

Luke 11:1-4

Bill Clinton was elected President of the United States in 1993. People throughout America discussed Clinton's political philosophy and their perception of his moral qualities. A widely known television preacher expressed grave concerns about Clinton's ability to lead the nation. At one point I remember the preacher saying, "What will become of the kingdom of God now." I could understand why so many people were discussing Clinton's political philosophy, but couldn't understand why anyone would think that the kingdom of God would come to an end because Bill Clinton became president. Did the preacher think Clinton's presidency was equal to the coronation as the king of God's kingdom? If he had mistaken the United States for the kingdom of God, he may not understand and embrace the fundamental doctrine of the Christian religion.

The kingdom of God is not a peripheral doctrine. One's view of the kingdom of God will have an influence over your Christian belief system. Of course, a kingdom presupposes a king. We cannot think of a king without thinking of the primary political motif for the greatest majority of human history. Furthermore, prayer is closely related to the kingdom of God, physically and spiritually.

In the English speaking Western world we've witnessed hundreds of years of monarchical rule in England. The principle title for the king of England is *Fidei Defensor*. (Defender of the faith) This was not merely a title. It explicitly intended to communicate that the king was God's political spokesman. The connection between the king and the church was complicated because the King established the religion of the land. If someone disagreed with the established religion, they were either persecuted or banished. One reason many fled to this country was to escape the established religion. The Puritans recognized the sphere sovereignty principle between the church and the state. The Puritans didn't separate the church and the state as we have seen in recent times in this country, because they acknowledged that above the state and the church was God. The kingdom of God is not exclusive. In fact, it includes the church and the state.

It is not my purpose to expound on the theories of the church and state, but I can say without reservation that the concept of the separation of church and state does not mean the separation of state and God. The modern notions of the separation of church and state come from the wicked worldview called secularism. Secularism is a worldview that teaches the state has no higher authority by which the state can be held accountable. Therefore the state becomes the moral standard by which laws are established. It is well known that a king demands obedience to his law.

The moral standard associated with God's law demands obedience from the citizens of this world. It is the imperfections of individual citizens that diffuse the kingdom regalia. The concept of "kingdom regalia" refers to the expressions of honor to the king through liturgical acts of worship and praise. Psalm 47 gives a better picture of kingdom regalia.

> Oh, clap your hands, all you peoples! Shout to God with the voice of triumph! For the LORD Most High is awesome; He is a great King over all the earth. He will subdue the peoples under us, and the nations under our feet. He will choose our inheritance for us, the excellence of Jacob whom He loves. Selah. God has

gone up with a shout, the LORD with the sound of a trumpet. Sing praises to God, sing praises! Sing praises to our King, sing praises! For God is the King of all the earth; Sing praises with understanding. God reigns over the nations; God sits on His holy throne. The princes of the people have gathered together, the people of the God of Abraham. For the shields of the earth belong to God; He is greatly exalted. (Psalm 47:1-9)

This royal Psalm expresses the activities of a particular feast day when God's people would gather to celebrate the coronation of God. Notice the figurative expressions of reality:

Clap hands is a sign the people welcome the advent of God's reign.

Shout to express the joy of God's awesome power.

King over all the earth.

God reigns over the nations.

The expressions of regalia absolutely demolish the idea of a tyrannical king. Unfortunately the concept of anti-sovereignty has taken its toll in western civilization over the past couple of hundred years. It was the righteous hatred of the established anti-sovereignty church by our godly forefathers that was perverted by our ungodly forefathers, thus the birth of anti-sovereignty in the American church. Once the seed of anti-sovereignty was planted the biblical concept of the kingdom of God became unpalatable to the culture at large. Your view of the kingdom of God will affect your view of the relationship between church and state. Your view of the kingdom of God will be reflected in your understanding of the second coming of Christ. If we ever expect to recover a proper understanding of the kingdom of God, we must pray thy kingdom come.

We all have questions about the kingdom of God. Who is this king and how does he govern his kingdom? And where is this kingdom located? When Jesus Christ explained to Pilate that the kingdom of God was not of this world, it confused Pilate. We are like Pilate in that we too think in terms of a kingdom exercising power and authority at the present time in this secular world. A king cannot be a king without being sovereign. A king is not a king unless he can exercise his dominion, power and authority over those in his kingdom. For example "thy kingdom" in the Lord's model prayer means the kingdom belongs to God. God is not just a shareholder; he is the owner, lock, stock, and barrel.

Since secularism has become the majority worldview in this country, the anti-sovereignty regime has infiltrated every aspect of church life, including prayer. Jesus taught his disciples to pray "thy kingdom come."

In the second petition the Lord Jesus Christ commands Christians to pray to the king in this manner: "thy kingdom come." The Lord not only commands them to pray in this manner, but the manner in which they pray is commanding. In biblical interpretation it may be referred to as an imperative of command or to put it another way it is treated like an injunction that calls for strict obedience. There is no ambiguity in the text concerning this command and we must humbly call on God to turn this command into reality.

The kingdom of God will always lead us to a human/divine relationship. God is a spirit, transcendent, holy, inscrutable, and incomprehensible. A Christian is a creature, limited in space and time, and a sinner, yet he has been adopted by the sovereign God. It is in the kingdom of God that man and God meet. When Jesus began his ministry in Galilee he said "The time is fulfilled, and the kingdom of God is at hand" (Mark 1:15). Then He made several other references to the kingdom of God.

> "Blessed are you poor, for yours is the kingdom of God" (Luke 6:20).

> "The kingdom of God has come near you" (Luke 10:9-11).

> "For indeed, the kingdom of God is within you" (Luke 17:21).

The kingdom of God has several dimensions. There is the political dimension, the economic dimension, the social dimension and so on. Although all those dimensions are important, we must begin our inquiry at the place we best understand the reign of God and that is in our hearts. When we pray for thy kingdom to come we are asking God to more and more establish his rule in our hearts. By establishing His rule in our hearts the mind, emotions and will become more and more God-centered rather than man-centered. The various dimensions of the kingdom of God will become important, if God rules in your heart. The kingdom of God will rule in the heart of men several different ways.

First, the kingdom of God will rule in your heart by way of truth. It may be said that the kingdom of God is the kingdom of truth. When Jesus was on trial before the Pontius Pilate the kingdom of God was the major subject.

> Pilate answered, "Am I a Jew? Your own nation and the chief priests have delivered You to me. What have you done?" Jesus answered, "My kingdom is not of this world. If My kingdom were of this world, My servants would fight, so that I should not be delivered to the Jews; but now My kingdom is not from here."

Pilate therefore said to Him "Are you a king then?" Jesus answered, "You say rightly that I am a king. For this cause I was born, and for this cause I have come into the world, that I should bear witness to the truth. Everyone who is of the truth hears my voice." (John 18:35-37)

The kingdom of God is the kingdom of truth. God is not confused and he cannot contradict himself. His kingdom is absolutely pure and not mixed with error. We pray for God's kingdom to come with pure truth. The truth begins with an understanding God's nature and character in comparison to man's depraved nature. The holiness of God is in contrast with the sinfulness of man. The power of God is in contrast to the weakness of man. The fullness of God is in contrast to the emptiness of man until God reveals and applies His saving truth to the soul of man. This truth is delivered to the hearts of men by the preaching of the Word of God and applied to the heart by the Holy Spirit. The kingdom of God is established by God's truth and yet today the majority of professing Christians do not believe there is any such thing as absolute truth. When you pray "thy kingdom come" are you praying for God's saving truth to reign in your heart?

The kingdom of God will also rule in your heart by way of grace. The kingdom of grace is the establishment of the new nature that brings light to the mind, order to the emotions, and surrender to the will. It is the kingdom of grace that announces to the world that you are a sinner saved by the perfect atoning sacrifice of Jesus Christ. When we pray "thy kingdom come" we are praying for the kingdom of grace to reign in hearts of Christians all over the earth.

Are you praying that the kingdom of God will come by way of grace so that your redemption will be made sure and that the gospel will be heard around the earth? The kingdom of God will not only rule in your heart by way of truth and grace, the kingdom of God will rule in the kingdom of glory. The kingdom of glory refers to the eternal Sabbath rest where the saints will reign with God and the angels forever. The kingdom of glory will be free from all the imperfections of our human nature and we will be endowed with the glorious perfections obtained for us by the Lord Jesus Christ. The kingdom of glory has no temptations, sorrows, or doubts. What it does have is the perfection of divine knowledge and immediate communion with God. When you pray "thy kingdom come" let your mind be set on Christ the king as you appear before him in eternal glory.

4. Pray for God's Will to Be Done

Your will be done…

Luke 11:1-4

God's will is inseparably connected with God's commandments. The Bible even mentions that angels obey the Lord. "Bless the Lord, you His angels, who excel in strength, who do his word" (Psalm 103:20). God's will is a primary and active component of God's activity in creation and providence. His activity in providence through second causes captures the attention of Christians and unbelievers. God's people pray for God's providential will to be done, because He is not only the Creator; He is provider, sustainer, and governor of His creation. Christians delight to see God's providential will in the history of the world.

God must reign in our hearts before the will becomes willing. Christians should take note of this portion of the Lord's model prayer relative to the human will. However, they must keep in mind that they are praying for God's will. God's will has two different perspectives.

First Christians pray for God's decretive will to be done. God's decretive will is His inscrutable counsel. Some of God's decrees are simply beyond human understanding. God's decrees cannot be resisted and are always fulfilled. Christians should desire that God's decrees will be fulfilled. God's decretive will refers to His holy will, because his decretive will is without sin.

Christians also pray that God's preceptive will be done. His preceptive will refers to the things that God wills by precept. In summary Christians are moral creatures and have been called to obey the precepts or the commandments of God. God's preceptive will stands in direct opposition to natural man's self-will. I'm referring to natural man after the sin of Adam. The Lord's model prayer calls for obedience to God (every command in Scripture) without opposition or reluctance. The duty is noble, but the will of man is sinful. This prayer takes us to the cross, because it shows the utter inability and absence of any desire to do the will of God.

The night before Jesus was crucified he prayed to His Father and said, "O My Father, if it is possible, let this cup pass from Me; nevertheless, not as I will, but as You will." Martin Luther said that "Never man feared death like this man, and this is why. His whole being shrank from it; yet his prayer remained 'not as I will, but as You will.'" Jesus Christ prayed for God's will knowing very well that the means of salvation for God's people depended totally on His sacrifice. Professing believers are driven to the cross pleading for mercy because of their fragile and helpless condition. Until believers realize how unwilling they are to obey the commandments of Christ, they will continue to make feeble and unacceptable attempts to obey Him.

The Apostle Paul explains the will in terms of a soul function. "I delight in the law of God according to the inward man" (Romans 7:22). The "inward man" or the "inner man" refers to the soul. Paul wanted the Ephesians, "to be strengthened with power through His Spirit in the inner man" (Ephesians 3:16). Since the soul and the will are inseparable, a brief definition is in order.

This word (soul) found often in the Old and New Testament describes the entity that essentially belongs to human beings forever. Historically western philosophy has treated the soul as a spiritual dimension of humanity. It appears that modern psychology locates the soul in some physical substance, since they often prescribe drugs that alter the brain function. Although theologians have serious disagreements on the meaning of the soul, a study of the full counsel of God will help define the meaning. The Bible uses the word "soul" to describe a person or a living being to establish a body/soul relationship. Although distinctions are made, the word may refer to material substance or a spiritual entity. For many theologians the soul, being a spiritual entity, is said to consist of the mind, will, and emotions.

A brief definition for the will:

> This aspect of the soul is that part that makes decisions relative to conditions and contingencies associated with the thinking mind. The will of God is perfect unlike the will of sinful man. Volition is the act of choice according to the prevailing good that comes from the result of the choice. (*Theological Terms in Layman Language*, by Martin Murphy, p. 109)

When you meet Jesus Christ at the cross, you will love to obey His commandments. You will cherish His commandments. However, the body (outward man) struggles against the soul (inward man). The Apostle Paul concludes: "But I see another law in my members, warring against the law of my mind, and bringing me into captivity to the law of sin which is in my members" (Romans 7:23). When Christians attempt to obey God out of an individualistic pious human attitude then there is no joy, no real sense of God's will being done.

The practice of true religion is found in the will of God. Christians must know God's will before they can do God's will. Numerous surveys conducted by Christian pollsters asked professing Christians the question: Can you name the Ten Commandments? Nearly 90% could not name the Ten Commandments and some could not name any of them. How on this earth can anyone with any integrity pray this prayer and command God's will to be done without having a clue as to what His will is? It is mockery to pray that God's will be done if God's will is not known.

Sound knowledge of what God expects is necessary to pray for God's will to be done. There are hundreds of commandments in Scripture. The Ten Commandments summarize the commandments in Scripture.

The sixth commandment is "you shall not murder." However, it refers to more than physical murder of the body. Disobedience proceeds from the soul by degrees. Jesus clarifies this doctrine.

> "You have heard that it was said to those of old, 'You shall not murder, and whoever murders will be in danger of the judgment.' But I say to you that whoever is angry with his brother without a cause shall be in danger of the judgment. And whoever says to his brother, 'Raca!' shall be in danger of the council. But whoever says, 'You fool!' shall be in danger of hell fire..." (Matthew 5:21-22)

Justifiable anger is evident if someone violates God's law. For instance, false teachers who teach false doctrine are liars. Unjustifiable anger occurs when someone says or does something that another person does not like, but it is not a violation of God's law. The Bible teaches that someone can murder a person's character by demonstrating an indifferent mean-spirited attitude expressed by malicious words.

The commandment "You shall not murder" has a wide range of applications. Professing Christians should endeavor to understand all the implications. For instance, did you know that if you destroy the name and reputation of someone without cause you will be in danger of eternal Hell? (See Matthew 5:21-26 for further study.) It is God's will for a converted sinner to abstain from damaging a person's character. I know plenty of people who have prayed the Lord's model prayer and yet they routinely criticize and demean other Christians without a biblical cause. Professing Christians have a duty to know God's will so they can do God's will. They should ask these questions:

1. Is my spiritual condition bad?
2. Do I want to know God's will for my life?
3. Do I want to understand what the Bible teaches?
4. Do I want God to reign in my heart?

So what should be done? Pray for God's will to be done. Pray that God will enable you to yield obedience to His will. Pray that God will remove your ignorance and blindness. Pray that you can see the beauty and glory of God's will.

Free will is a subject that conducts plenty of heat without accomplishing anything. Professing Christians should spend more time learning and submitting to God's will. They must know God's will before they can do it. They must submit to God's will in order to do it.

Christians cling to the cross when they pray "Your will be done." Without the cross and the atoning work of Jesus Christ, professing Christians do not want to know God's will even though it is apparent. Without understanding the sacrifice of Jesus Christ on the cross, professing Christians cannot submit to God's will. However, Christians will desire to submit to God's will if the kingdom of God reigns in their heart.

God promised to put His Spirit within His people and then God would cause them to walk in His statutes. Christians can only submit to Christ and obey Him if His Spirit transforms them and causes them to obey Him.

Submission to God's will does not occur merely from a dread of punishment or fear of His wrath. Christians submit to God because they love Him and His ways. Humility is the first step toward submission to God. Pride is the root cause of disobedience to God's will, because a proud man thinks it is below him to stoop to God's will.

There are many reasons why Christians should humble themselves and submit to God's will.

1. God's will is sovereign. (Humility is necessary.)

2. God's will is wise. (Your intellectual capacity can't compare.)

3. God's will is just. (God's justice is perfect.)

4. God's will is gracious. (God's will is not a burden.)

If you know God's will and submit to God's will, then God's will be done in the manner in which God wants it done. "Your will be done on earth as it is in heaven." This does not refer to a perfect heavenly state. The word "as" refers to similitude, not equality.

The saints on earth are to do the will of God in a similar manner that the inhabitants of heaven do God's will. Like the angels in heaven, Christians on earth demonstrate faithfulness, zeal and passion for God's will, and sincerity in worship and service.

When you pray "Your will be done" are you prepared to do what is necessary to know God's will? When you pray "Your will be done" are you prepared to submit to God's will?

5. Pray: Give Us Day by Day Our Daily Bread

Give us day by day our daily bread...

Luke 11:1-4

There are two parts to the Lord's model prayer. The first part directs attention to the nature and character of the triune God. The second part directs attention to the needs of God's children. So it would seem logical that one half the prayer time should be spent talking to God about God. God's glory is first in importance and should require a major portion of prayer time.

The Lord's model prayer is a prayer for professing Christians only, because it is only professing Christians who can delight in God's glory, majesty, dignity, love, justice, holiness, truth, wisdom, power, goodness, Excellences, perfections, and mercy.

A child loves his father and wants to know everything about his father. A child loves his father and wants to please his father. Those principles apply to the Lord's model prayer. Christians love their heavenly Father and they reverently honor and cherish His name above all other names. Christians love their heavenly Father and they desire for Him to reign over their lives. Since Christians love their heavenly Father, they want to do his will.

This present world with all its gold and glitter becomes dim as we behold the glory of our Father in heaven. Christians cannot pray without thinking of the glory of God. However, the Lord's model prayer includes the needs of God's children, but even their needs reflect the glory of God. The Lord's model prayer instructs the people of God to ask the Lord to provide daily bread day by day. The poor man may think this prayer is specifically for him since he needs bread to survive. The rich man may think this prayer does not apply to him. However, the ultimate source of all earthly needs and wealth is from the Lord God Almighty.

When Christians pray "Give us this day our bread" they are not praying to a confused deity who is unaware of their needs. God created them and He sustains, provides, and governs them because He knew beforehand what they would need. Everything is a gift from God.

Christians pray for God to supply daily bread day by day when the pantry is empty because the Lord is concerned for our bodily needs. Jesus fed 5000 people on one occasion because He was concerned for their bodily needs. Your body is part of God's good creation and you can honor the Lord by having an interest in your bodily needs.

Christians pray to God and say "Give us" because God is not weary of providing for His people. His mercy endures forever. God delights in giving. A good father delights in giving to His children.

You ask for God to provide for your needs and He provides, but why? Why do you ask and why does God provide? The answer is the child of God desires temporal resources for spiritual ends. They pray for food, health, strength, and wisdom, because these things are necessary to sustain them on their trip to heaven. The people of God are sojourners in the wilderness. They are on the way to "the city which has foundations, whose builder and maker is God" (Hebrews 11:10).

If a person has a rich and abundant estate, should that person pray and say, "Give us daily bread?" The answer is a resounding yes. If God should withhold his blessing, all the material wealth in the world serves no purpose. When the Israelites complained because they had no meat in the wilderness, God sent quail in abundance, but the Bible explains, "while the meat was still between their teeth, before it was chewed, the wrath of the Lord was aroused against the people and the Lord struck the people with a very great plague" (Numbers 11:33). Plenty of money, or a freezer full of food, or a barn full of hay, doesn't insure God's blessing. If you have all these things and God does not bless them to your good, they will only hasten your misery and death. Rich or poor, we must all ask God to give us our daily bread.

The Lord's model prayer is very specific relative to our daily needs. The Lord instructs His church to pray, "Give us day by day our daily bread." Notice the phrase "day by day." The Greek word *epiousios* translates to English "day by day." This is a rare Greek word. It is only used in the Lord's model prayer in the entire Bible and rarely out of Scripture. I translate from the Greek in this manner: "Give us according to our existence each day daily bread." We are asking God to provide for us according to our numbered days on earth.

Christians humbly and with moderation in mind request those things they need, because they trust the Lord God who provides daily existence. Christians should ask God enough for each day and live as if each day was our last day on earth. The Lord instructs Christians to pray for "our bread." The prayer is not for "my bread." It is "our bread" and therefore showing an unselfish desire for God to supply the collective church with daily needs.

The Lord's model prayer begins with "our Father." The church collectively enjoys the glorious name, rule, and will of "our Father." The consensus of unity belongs to the church. The word bread refers to all the temporal blessings of this life. "Whatever serves for our well-being" was the way St. Augustine understood "our bread."

Jesus may have been thinking of the prayer in Proverbs. "Give me neither poverty nor riches – Feed me with the food allotted to me" (Proverbs 30:8). Our daily bread refers to those material things that God allots to us as we need them.

Some people need more material things that other people. For example, Eskimos living in a freezing climate will need more clothes than man living in Key West, Florida. The owner of a furniture store needs more capital for investment and expansion than the salesman in the furniture store. But there are some people who want and take more material things than they need. They crave material things like an alcoholic craves liquor. It is a sign of a covetous heart. Covetousness is a root sin or a radical sin. Covetousness is a desire to obtain an excessive amount of material things. As the Puritan Thomas Watson wrote, "Covetousness is not only in getting riches unjustly, but in loving them inordinately...." Covetousness is the root cause for theft. It may evidence itself by robbing a bank. Covetousness may evidence itself by taking advantage of another person's inadequacy or circumstances. Covetousness causes treason and murder. It is also the spring of apostasy. The apostle Paul said, "Demas has forsaken me having loved this present world." The Lord's model prayer instructs Christians to turn away from the awful sin of covetousness.

Christians must be content with "our daily bread" because God can bless a small amount. If God keeps us from the plenitude of worldly things, He may very well make up for it by giving us spiritual growth, which is eternally more important than temporal things. If you have less daily bread than the next person, you will have less to give account for when you stand before God. "For everyone to whom much is given, from him much will be required; and to whom much has been committed, of him they will ask the more" (Luke 12:48).

The doctrine of God's providence and Christian stewardship are inseparably connected in this portion of the Lord's model prayer. Under the inspiration of God, the Apostle Paul reminds us to "Be anxious for nothing, but in everything by prayer and supplication with thanksgiving, let your requests be made known to God;" Paul goes on to say "God shall supply all your needs according to His riches in glory by Christ Jesus."

The application of the redemptive work of Jesus Christ to your heart is the only way that you can truly pray "Give us day by day our daily bread." The Lord's model prayer is the perfect objective standard to teach you to pray day by day for your daily bread.

6. Pray: Forgive Our Sins

And forgive us our sins, for we also forgive everyone who is indebted to us...

Luke 11:1-4

Since the Lord's model prayer for Christians is brief, it will be wise to carefully examine the content. The Lord instructs us to pray for daily bread to sustain bodily life before He mentioned forgiveness, a necessary condition for the good health of the soul. We are instructed to pray daily for daily needs, but we must not forget that when we pray for daily bread we are praying for God's provision for both body and soul. Prayer for our soul has eternal consequences. "For what profit is it to a man if he gains the whole world, and loses his own soul" (Matthew 16:26)? The body needs bread for this life, but the soul needs forgiveness of sin for the life to come.

There are some minor differences in the use of words and the grammar of Matthew's account of the Lord's model prayer and Luke's account of the Lord's model prayer. The Matthew text is, "And forgive us our debts, as we forgive our debtors" (Matthew 6:12). The word debt is taken from a Greek word that means to owe something. The Luke text is, "And forgive us our sins, for we also forgive everyone who is indebted to us" (Luke 11:6). The word "sin" is taken from a Greek word that means to miss God's absolute standard of perfection. Some people/congregations repeat the Lord's model prayer during worship services. Some churches use the word "trespass" in the place of debt: "Forgive us our trespasses as we forgive those who trespass against us." However, Christians should remember that sin refers to "unpaid debts." The simple words in the Lord's model prayer are, "Forgive us our sins."

In a postmodern culture sin is not an acceptable expression of human condition. The therapeutic industry has consumed the church with unbiblical solutions to resolving broken relationships. Now the church has a problem grasping the seriousness of sins or as the Lord says "our debts." What are "our sins?"

> We sin by breaking the law of God.
> We sin when we deviate from God's standards.
> We sin by missing the mark of perfection.
> We sin by rebelling against God.

Professing Christians must come to grips with the holiness of God and sinfulness of mankind.

> The horrifying result of the sin of our first parents is not just death, but the total depravity that accompanies the death. Total depravity means that man is "wholly defiled in all the faculties and parts of soul and body." The soul consists of the mind, will, and emotions. The mind of man, being the center of his intellect, was darkened so that the moral and natural abilities of the intellect were diminished. The mind was not destroyed, but it was "defiled." The will of man once faithful to God became rebellious and capricious. The affections once harmonious and delighted in the beauty of God became deranged and inflamed with pride, lust, and covetousness. Paul the Apostle describes the condition of the human race as being dead in trespasses and sin. (*Doctrine of Sound Words: Summary of Christian Theology*, by Martin Murphy, p.40)

The Bible explains the standard. "For whoever shall keep the whole law and yet stumble in one point he is guilty of all" (James 2:10). James must mean that when we commit the least sin we are sinning against the law-Maker who gave us the whole law. King David cried out to God, "Against You, You only, have I sinned" (Psalm 51:4). David sinned against Bethsheba by committing adultery. David sinned against Uriah by having him murdered. (See 2 Samuel 11:2-25 for the entire event.)

David's primary root sin was against God who created Bathsheba and Uriah. God established an absolute standard for community life among the covenant people of God that David violated. David's only hope was for God to show compassion, grace and mercy, declare him righteous, and forgive his sin. It is your only hope and my only hope.

The debt we owe God for all the sins we've committed in thought, word, and deed is immeasurable. The Lord's model prayer drives us to the cross because our sin debt is so great we can't possibly pay it.

Professing Christians are easily distracted from their sin debt to God. However, a five minute examination will reveal their sin debts. The first commandment requires perfect knowledge of God, acknowledge all His perfections, and never worship false gods. The second commandment defines the manner of worship required by God. If we fail to worship the way God commands, we deserve nothing less than the same punishment received by Nadab and Abihu (Leviticus 10:1-2). The third commandment is the law of reverence. It calls us to revere God's name above all other names. Any lack of understanding the name of God and thus the character of God is a violation of this commandment. The fourth commandment is virtually ignored in the modern church. The commandment calls each man to work hard six days and keep the Sabbath holy unto the Lord. The law of authority comes next exemplified by the commandment to honor thy father and mother. Our sin debt to God also includes murder, adultery, theft, lying, and covetousness. A brief analysis of your sin debt will overwhelm you. The sin debt is beyond your capacity to pay it. There is only one way for your sin debt to be paid and that is by the pledge of someone who is able to pay your debt. It is Jesus Christ and His life giving grace that will save you.

Sin is not just an act; it is part of the human personality. The guilt of sin is inherited. Sin causes guilt, guilt causes hatred, and hatred causes murder. God can forgive sin, and by forgiving sin the guilt is removed and when the guilt is removed, hatred will turn into mercy and compassion.

If you carry the burden of guilt, I plead with you to plead with the Lord God omnipotent for the forgiveness of your sin and sins and the removal of guilt though the shed blood of the Lord Jesus Christ. Ask God the Holy Spirit to send comfort and joy to your soul.

I have never personally heard of a Christian refusing to ask God forgiveness for sins against Him, but the next part of the Lord's Prayer may not be received with as much enthusiasm: "For we also forgive everyone who is indebted to us." I personally know Christians who have offended and sinned against other Christians and have not asked for forgiveness, which means a debt remains unpaid.

Understanding the importance of the word "debt" becomes exceedingly important. If someone sins against you that person has an obligation to you or to put it another way that person has a debt to pay. You must of necessity forgive that debt, if the debtor asks forgiveness. This "debt" does not refer to a financial transaction between Christians and it does not mean that they earn God's forgiveness by forgiving someone else.

Forgiveness in this text is more correctly understood as evidence of a spiritual condition, than a qualification for forgiveness by God. God, by His pure grace, forgives you of your multiplied sins against Him. Then you likewise, by grace, forgive your Christian brother or sister. When you forgive, truly forgive, you are simply following the example of your

Lord and give evidence of the grace of the Lord Jesus Christ present in your soul.

If you are not able to forgive others who have sinned against you, then you have not received any forgiveness from God. I know this is hard, but these are not my words. They come directly from the mouth of the Lord. Matthew and Luke give an account of the Lord's model prayer. Although they include the doctrine of forgiveness, according to Matthew's account the Lord clarifies the doctrine of forgiveness. "For if you forgive men their trespasses, your heavenly Father will also forgive you. But if you do not forgive men their trespasses, neither will your Father forgive your trespasses" (Matthew 6:14-15). First the Lord addresses it positively: "For if you forgive men their trespasses, your heavenly Father will also forgive you." Then the Lord addresses it negatively: "But if you do not forgive men their trespasses, neither will your Father forgive your trespasses.

This does not mean that God's forgiveness is contingent upon your forgiving another person. It does mean that you will be compelled to forgive the other person if God has forgiven you. As Calvin so correctly says, "if the Spirit of God reigns in our hearts, every description of ill-will and revenge ought to be banished" (Calvin's Commentary on the Gospel of Luke).

You might be asking, "What must I do to forgive someone who has treated me unjustly?" John Calvin offers an excellent answer.

> This, rather, is our forgiveness: "willingly to cast from the mind wrath, hatred, desire for revenge, and willingly to banish to oblivion the remembrance of injustice. For this reason, we ought not to seek forgiveness of sins from God unless we ourselves also forgive the offenses against us of all those who do or have done us ill. If we retain feelings of hatred in our

hearts, if we plot revenge and ponder any occasion to cause harm and even if we do not try to get back into our enemies' good graces....and commend ourselves to them, by this prayer we entreat God not to forgive our sins. For we ask that God does to us as we do to others. (*Institutes of the Christian Religion*, by John Calvin, 3.20.45)

The instruction from the Lord is easy to understand. God forgives us and we also forgive everyone who is indebted to us. The manner in which we forgive is regulated by Scripture.

Forgiveness must come from the heart. "So My heavenly Father also will do to you if each of you, from his heart, does not forgive his brother his trespasses" (Matthew 18:35). (Also see Zechariah 8:16-17.)

Forgiveness must include full forgiveness. "As far as the east is from the west, so far has He removed our transgressions from us" (Psalm 103:12).

Forgiveness is a continuous discipline. "We also forgive everyone" (Luke 11:4). The Greek grammar indicates a statement of reality with ongoing action.

There are other factors that play into the biblical doctrine on forgiveness:

Matthew 5:21-26 teaches reconciliation before the judgment day.

Matthew 18:15-17 teaches reconciliation in the church.

Christians pray for forgiveness because God commands it;

Christians need to experience it. Prayer without understanding the content will surely bring a curse. If you pray according to the Lord's model prayer and mean every word of it, it will surely bring a blessing to your life.

7. Pray: Lead Us Not Into Temptation

*And do not lead us into temptation, but deliver us from the evil
one...*

Luke 11:1-4

The Lord's model prayer illustrates the content of our
spiritual discussion with God. The Lord's model prayer
expresses the comprehensive relationship between God and
man. It teaches believers how to maintain dignity and truth
when they go before the throne of grace.

The Lord instructs his church to pray for spiritual guidance
as each one faces temptation. For that reason, we ask our
Father in heaven to lead us not into temptation. The meaning
of the word temptation in the context of the Lord's Prayer
needs some explanation. A few verses from the book of James
will help us understand.

> Blessed is the man who endures temptation; for when
> he has been approved, he will receive the crown of life,
> which the Lord has promised to those who love Him.
> Let no one say when he is tempted, "I am tempted by
> God;" for God cannot be tempted by evil, nor does He
> Himself tempt anyone. But each one is tempted when
> he is drawn away by his own desires and enticed.
> (James 1:12-14)

God does not tempt anyone with evil because God is
absolutely holy. Trials, testing and temptations are common
to professing Christians. "My brethren, count it all joy when
you fall into various trials, knowing that the testing of your
faith produces patience" (James 1:2-3). The Christian life is
full of trials. The inspired Word of God in the book of James

is not ambiguous. If you are a Christian you will face trials. Paul explains the relationship of living godly lives and persecution, which is a trial that leads to temptation. "All who desire to live godly in Christ Jesus will be persecuted" (2 Timothy 2:12). Christians must face trials and temptations with an attitude of prayer.

Jesus instructs Christians to pray saying, "do not lead us into temptation, but deliver us from the evil one." This is a command of entreaty. The Greek grammar has the Christian literally begging God not to lead him or her into temptation. Christians are constantly on trial in this sinful world. However, they should pray that God will not let the trial turn into a temptation. The Bible teaches:

> No temptation has overtaken you except such as is common to man; but God is faithful, who will not allow you to be tempted beyond what you are able, but with the temptation will also make the way of escape. (1 Corinthians 10:13)

Since God cannot tempt us with evil, what is the sensible understanding of our text when we ask God not to lead us into temptation? We are asking God not to allow us to be drawn into our own evil inclinations or Satan's deceptive power. Evil inclinations derive from the natural sinful constitution often referred to as the "flesh." Jesus referred to the flesh just before he was arrested in the garden of Gethsemane.

> Then He came to the disciples and found them sleeping, and said to Peter, "What! Could you not watch with Me one hour? Watch and pray, lest you enter into temptation. The spirit indeed is willing, but the flesh is weak" (Matthew 26:40-41).

Paul discusses the work of the flesh in his letter to the

Galatians. They may be summarized as: resentment, revenge, injustice, oppression and distrust of God's providence (Galatians 5:19-21). The flesh is the source of evil thoughts, desires, and immoral actions that come from within. The inclination to sin is the natural condition of all rational beings, after the fall. Although faith in Christ restores a right relationship with God, the believer is not free from sin. However, a true child of God is less and less inclined to sin and actually hates his sins, but sin is still present in the inward man. Evil thoughts, desires, and actions also come from the temptations of Satan. For the good of your own soul ask God to keep you from the power of temptation from evil things and the evil one.

However, God may test you for the good of your own soul. God tested Abraham by instructing Abraham to sacrifice his son Isaac and after Abraham passed the test God promised Abraham a great blessing. God allowed Job to be tested. Jesus Christ was tested by Satan. We may be tested; therefore, we pray, "do not lead us into temptation." The Christian's petition is that evil will not prevail.

It has been said that "life is a spiritual battlefield" and the trials of life are good for the soul, so why should we pray for God not to lead us into temptation? The answer comes in remembering that the things God gives us for our good is used by Satan to try to hurt us.

The Lord's model prayer found in Matthew's gospel associates temptation with the tempter. The Bible teaches us that Satan is the one who deceives the whole world (Revelation 12:9). Satan will take every situation and try to mislead you with his lies. He will begin with your mind. An idle mind is the Devil's playground. If you empty yourself of the knowledge of God, Satan will tempt you to worship the creature rather than the Creator.

God will give you every opportunity to study His Word, but you must pray that you will not fall into temptation and allow Satan to convince you not to spend time reading and examining the Word of God, meditating upon it, and praying according to the Lord's model prayer. God urges you to examine yourself, but you must pray that you will not fall into temptation by Satan and his scheme to try and convince you not to examine the state of your soul.

God expects you to love the truth and have a passion for truth. If you have a passion for truth, pray for God not to lead you into temptation. Satan will do everything in his power to deceive you with lies on top of lies. Satan comes as an angel of light filling the minds of unsuspecting Christians with false religion. False religion is an error that spreads like the plague. Dr. Harold Parker has said, "error lies in the tendency for the student to follow the authority ahead of him in Indian file, deeper and deeper into the morass of error." False religion produces error which causes division in the church and hinders the work of reformation, because we do not pray and ask God not to lead us into temptation.

The temptation to sin is ever present because of your own inclination to sin. It is Satan who will capitalize upon your inclinations and bring about the finished work. Satan would lead you to believe your grace is superabundant. Peter said, "Lord I will not forsake you." Peter was boasting in his own power, but Peter fell prey to Satan. Satan will lead you to believe material things will solve your problems. Satan will lead you to believe that your way is the best way. How can you overcome these traps set by Satan? Pray that God will not allow these temptations to overcome you. Satan will endeavor to produce and strengthen the habit of sin. He will deceive you to turn a lesser sin into a greater sin. Satan may tempt you, but Satan cannot force your will.

Another source of temptation is the world. The good things of this world may become a snare and lead you into temptation. The pursuit of worldly gain to the exclusion of your spiritual sojourn may become a temptation to suppress

God's truth and serve the creature rather than the Creator. Overindulgence in food, drink, and recreation may tempt you to disregard the glory of God.

Paul's letter to Timothy reminds us of the many temptations that Christians face.

> But know this, that in the last days perilous times will come: For men will be lovers of themselves, lovers of money, boasters, proud, blasphemers, disobedient to parents, unthankful, unholy, unloving, unforgiving, slanderers, without self-control, brutal, despisers of good, traitors, headstrong, haughty, lovers of pleasure rather than lovers of God, having a form of godliness but denying its power. And from such people turn away! For of this sort are those who creep into households and make captives of gullible women loaded down with sins, led away by various lusts, always learning and never able to come to the knowledge of the truth. (2 Timothy 3:1-7)

Does the force of temptation cause you wonder about your relationship with Jesus Christ? Then run to the cross of Jesus Christ and cling to it. If you are one of God's children, it is impossible not be a child of God. Though you may fall by a temptation of some sort, the seed of God is in you (1 John 3:9). Though you may be overcome in a battle that does not mean you have lost the war. God does not judge his children by a moment of failure, but by the condition of their heart. If your heart is renewed by the power of the Holy Spirit then you should watch and pray that you may not enter into temptation;

When you pray the Lord's model prayer, pray with an earnest passion because the Bible teaches us to:

Ask and it will be given

Martin Murphy

Seek and you will find
Knock and it will be opened to you.

Your heavenly Father will give the Holy Spirit to you, but
you must pray that you will not be overtaken by temptation.

8. Pray for One Another

Confess your trespasses to one another, and pray for one another, that you may be healed. The effective, fervent prayer of a righteous man avails much.

James 5:16

The Christian doctrine of prayer is abundantly present in the Bible. However, the practice of the doctrine is in need of reformation. The basic meaning of the word "pray" or "prayer" is to call on God or go before God in confession, praise, thanksgiving and petition.

My observation on social media relative to the doctrine and practice of prayer does not generally conduce to the biblical doctrine. For instance, I read a local discussion board to get an idea of what the local people are thinking on issues. There have been numerous reports of families suffering a disaster. The immediate response from many on that discussion board is a caption like "prayers up" or simply "praying." Before suggesting this is a good and proper response, consider the context. Many of them have religious discussions occasionally and they mock the church and Christianity. Many of them smell of atheism or agnosticism at best. Yet they treat God like they would a vending machine. They insert their "prayers up" and expect the dispenser to furnish the product.

The Lord's model prayer is sufficient to instruct Christians in the doctrine, manner, and practice of their private and public prayer life. Unfortunately, many professing Christians do not like theological and doctrinal models. Too often they prefer their own private model. The Lord Jesus Christ faced death on the cross and prayed, "nevertheless, not as I will, but as You will" (Matthew 26:39).

Although the Lord's model prayer does not say "pray for one another," the language certainly implies that Christians must "pray for one another." A brief examination of the text will reveal the implied doctrine, "pray for one another."

> Luke 11:2 – "When you pray..." is the instruction from our Lord to His disciples. "You" is plural (you all), therefore it refers to all the disciples of Christ.

> Luke 11:2 – "Our Father" makes the obvious assertion that all the disciples are in a spiritual relation to one another.

> Luke 11:3 – "Give us" obviously means Christians are praying for one another in the spiritual family.

There is plenty of scriptural evidence indicating Christians should pray for one another. Prayer may be offered for individual Christians or for the church collectively. Prayer for one another is a doctrine that may be found in the Old and New Testament.

> Genesis 25:21 - Isaac prayed to the Lord on behalf of his wife, because she was barren. The Lord answered his prayer and his wife Rebekah became pregnant.

> 2 Chronicles 30:18 - Hezekiah prayed for the people: May the Lord, who is good, pardon everyone who sets his heart on seeking God . . . . even if he is not clean according to the rules of the sanctuary. And the Lord heard Hezekiah and healed the people [made them ceremonially clean].

> Psalm 122:6 – Pray for the peace of Jerusalem.

Jeremiah 7:16 – Therefore do not pray for this people, nor lift up a cry or prayer for them, nor make intercession to Me; for I will not hear you.

Acts 13:2-3 - As they ministered to the Lord and fasted, the Holy Spirit said, "Now separate to Me Barnabas and Saul for the work to which I have called them." Then, having fasted and prayed, and laid hands on them, they sent them away.

The doctrine of intercession has been mistakenly used in relation to the doctrine of praying for one another. The doctrine of intercession refers to prayer offered by Christ for all who truly belong to Him. This prayer is offered only from the sinless perfect Mediator to God the Father. "Therefore He is also able to save to the uttermost those who come to God through Him, since He always lives to make intercession for them" (Hebrews 7:25). One sinful Christian human being cannot intercede for another sinful Christian human being.

Christians pray for God's providential care; however, request and petitions must be agreeable to the will of God. There are times when it is a sin to pray. Such occasions are not agreeable with the will of God. "If you hold anything against anyone, forgive him so that your Father in heaven may forgive you your sins" (Mark 11:25). There is a little mentioned Psalm that Christians ought to remember. "If I had cherished sin in my heart, the Lord would not have listened" (Psalm 66:18). God will not hear the prayers of an unregenerate heart. Self-examination, confession of sin, and repentance precedes prayer for one another. God will not hear the prayer of a rebellious Christian. God will not listen to hypocritical prayers. "When you spread out your hands in prayer, I will hide my eyes from you even if you offer many prayers, I will not listen" (Isaiah 1:15).

There are times when it is a sin not to pray. Samuel

realized the need to pray for the people of God. "As for me, far be it from me that I should sin against the Lord by failing to pray for you" (1 Samuel 12:23).

Scripture teaches that it is good to pray for anyone in the family of God. James expresses that general principle in the inspired Word. "Anyone, then, who knows the good he ought to do and doesn't do it sins" (James 4:17). Paul applies that principle to prayer. "I urge, then first of all, that request, prayers, intercession and thanksgiving be made for everyone" (1 Timothy 2:1).

The consequences of not praying for one another in the household of God may devastate the family of God. In the Old Testament the people of God were called Israel. In the New Testament the people of God are called the church. God warned the Old Testament congregation, for nearly six hundred years to repent and return to Him. They had departed from true worship to false worship and false gods. Obviously, prayers were offered to false gods. The Old Testament congregation was taken captive by the Babylonians. This is a notable example of God's people not understanding the necessity of true prayer to the true God.

Christians should pray for one another on a regular basis. Paul told the Thessalonians to "pray without ceasing" (1 Thessalonians 5:17). I've heard Christians say something to the effect, "I have to work, eat, and sleep. I can't pray all the time." The New Testament was originally written in the Greek language. Some English Bible translations are accurate so far as translating word for word. However, there are a few occasions that leave the text ambiguous to the reader. This is one of them. The word "pray" is a present imperative verb. It means the action is a command and it is ongoing in the present time. In English the tense stresses the time of the action. In Greek the tense stresses the kind of action. Greek grammar refers to the action in this verse as the iterative present tense. To put it another way, it is an action that is repeated over and over. I try to stay away from the Greek/English stuff, but I didn't know how to explain this without explaining it!

Prayer for one another indicates an interest in each other's sanctification. (I devoted chapter 10 to a discussion of sanctification.) The word sanctification explains the progressive work of growing in holiness and grace. The process is a lifetime exercise. The doctrine of sanctification is about living unto righteousness and freeing us from sinful behavior. Praying for a brother or sister in Christ, who is struggling with sin, is noble and loving. Pray with reverence to God. Let your mind turn toward God. Pray with a sense of unworthiness as Calvin wrote, "Let each one, therefore, as he prepares to pray be displeased with his own evil deeds, and ...let him take the person and disposition of a beggar." Pray for the forgiveness of sin. Pray with confidence.

Prayer should drive Christians to action. Let me illustrate with this brief story. Two friends were discussing each other's needs. They decided to pray for each other. After a brief time of prayer one friend asked the other. "If you had a million dollars would you give me half of it?" His friend answered, "Yes I would." The next question was, "if you had two Cadillac's would you give me one?" His friend answered, "Yes I would." The final question was, "if you had two cows would you give me one?" His friend responded, "You know I've got two cows!"

"He answered and said to them, 'He who has two tunics, let him give to him who has none; and he who has food, let him do likewise'" (Luke 3:11).

9. Prayer for Salvation

Brethren, my heart's desire and prayer to God for Israel is that they may be saved...

Romans 10:1

Salvation has come to the Gentiles...

Romans 11:11

The Apostle Paul was a man of prayer. He made prayer a regular part of his Christian experience. Paul's rich doctrine of prayer reveals his purpose for prayer. Paul prayed intelligently, consistently, and continually.

Paul was an evangelist and preacher, but he was also a pastor. As a pastor he loved the church of God. You can't love the church without loving the people in the church. I hope you are not deceived by the use of the word love. It is not a word that merely describes an emotional response one person has for another. Love has the best interest of the loved at heart. True love touches the whole soul, the mind, the will and the emotions. Paul loved the church even though it had members who acted very ungodly. Paul also loved those outside the church, even those who despised the law and the gospel.

Paul wrote a letter to the church at Rome to let them know that he was "not ashamed of the gospel of Christ for it is the power of God to salvation for everyone who believes" (Romans. 1:16). A brief summary of Paul's letter to the Romans reveals his passion for the salvation of God's people. Paul deals with theological issues concerning the salvation of God's elect in Chapters 1-8. Although it is virtually impossible to give a brief summary of Paul's theology from these chapters, Romans 8:30 probably does it the best. "Moreover whom He predestined, these He also called; whom He called, these He also justified; and whom He justified, these He also glorified." Then in Chapters 9-11 Paul expresses his sorrow for his fellow countrymen who failed to understand that God is absolutely sovereign.

Paul is first concerned that God's sovereignty not be violated. He said: "Does not the potter have the right to make out of the same lump of clay one vessel for honor and another for dishonor" (Romans 9:19-29)? Paul concludes that "he who puts his faith in Christ will not be put to shame" (Romans 9:30-33). Paul's exposition in chapters one through nine probes some of the most complicated doctrine in Scripture. Paul teaches that sinful man seeks to establish his own righteousness.

When a pastor watches professing Christians violate the Word of God and seek to establish their own righteousness and salvation, it can be very painful. The pastor knows he has no power to save the souls that God has put under the pastor's care. Furthermore, the pastor is aware he has no power to save the soul of someone outside the fellowship of the church. So what did pastor Paul do even though he concluded that all human beings, especially those we care about, whether they are in the church or out of the church, are in need of God's saving grace? What does the pastor do when he knows they are hopeless without the righteousness of Christ?

Godly pastors pray for the salvation of the unsaved. Prayer ought to precede the evangelistic enterprise. Unfortunately many evangelicals today suppose unsaved individuals can be converted by following a certain plan or by devising a method that will cause someone to accept Christ. However, those ideas are not taught in Scripture. Scripture does teach Christians to have a passion for the salvation of the lost and pray for their salvation. The book of Romans is timely for those who believe in praying for the salvation of lost sinners.

Romans is the great theological book in the Bible. The doctrines of original sin, regeneration, justification, adoption, and sanctification are carefully outlined, not to mention the rarely mentioned doctrines in the church such as predestination and election. Even so the Bible uses those words often. Many professing Christians believe that election and predestination are barriers to evangelism. Paul certainly didn't think so. Predestination is no barrier to evangelism. Predestination by a sovereign God ought to be the stimulating factor to pray for the salvation of those whom God has called to himself. Our attitude toward men is not to be governed by God's secret counsel concerning them. We must be like the Apostle Paul. We must have as our "heart's desire" the salvation of lost sinners. If the "heart's desire" is to save the lost then by all means pray for them by name.

Your passion to pray for the lost sinner will increase as you understand the sovereignty of God. Even if we arouse all our passions and pray for the lost, we must direct our prayers to God who provides salvation for the lost. When the Ark of the Lord was returned to Jerusalem after the Philistines were defeated, David said in his prayer of thanksgiving "Save us, O God of our salvation... (1 Chronicles 16:35). When David prayed his prayer of repentance in Psalm 51 he said, "Deliver me from the guilt of bloodshed, O God, The God of my salvation. . ." (Psalm 51:14).

Over and over again the Bible uses the same language: "the God of my salvation." Professing Christians ignore the clear doctrine of Scripture to their own peril. God justifies some according to the righteousness of Christ. He not only justifies, God sanctifies some for His good pleasure. Finally, God will glorify some for His own glory.

Professing Christians would run away from man-made methods of evangelism and return to biblical standards, if they understood the saving grace of God working in the lives of men, women and children.

If the Bible abundantly and clearly explains the doctrine of salvation, then salvation is something that God the Father,

God the Son, and God the Holy Spirit does for His own glory. If our salvation is from God, then we must pray to Him for salvation. Every Christian believer is able to be part of the great evangelistic enterprise by praying to God for the salvation of particular people.

It is not merely the duty of the pastor to offer up prayers for salvation, it is the duty of all Christians to pray for the salvation of sinners. Prayer for the salvation of the lost is specifically a duty for all spiritual patriots. Paul told the Thessalonian church and by extension and application he speaks to the church in all ages that they must pray always. Paul said "pray without ceasing" because prayer is the will of God in Christ (1 Thessalonians 5:17).

Paul referred to the Christians at the church of Rome as brethren. It was Paul's way of calling the whole church to this noble work. It is a reflection of Paul's charged emotions and affection for those who are without the righteousness of Christ, whether in the church or out of the church.

Paul's spiritual patriotism is reflected by "his heart's desire and prayer to God" for his fellow countrymen. The highest good you can hope for your loved one or friend is the salvation of his or her soul; even more so for your enemy. The best thing that could ever happen to your enemy is to be converted to the Christian religion. He or she would no longer be your enemy, but a brother or sister. This unique relationship brings unity to the church. Paul explains this doctrine.

> Therefore if there is any consolation in Christ, if any comfort of love, if any fellowship of the Spirit, if any affection and mercy, fulfill my joy by being like-minded, having the same love, being of one accord, of one mind. (Philippians 2:1-2)

Prayer for the salvation of a lost soul reveals a heart of

mercy, compassion, and love. Christians ought to pray for God to open the spiritual eyes of the unbeliever so they may understand the righteousness of Christ and believe it. Of course they cannot see the righteousness of Christ until they see the depravity of their sin. So pray that they will see their depraved nature and that God would save them in spite of their depravity. Pray that they would stop seeking to establish their own righteousness and their ignorance of God's righteousness will be removed. Pray that they will confess with their mouth that Jesus Christ is Lord and believe in their heart that God has raised Him from the dead. Pray that God would send a preacher and that the preacher will preach the gospel of peace. Pray that God will send a teacher that will teach the full counsel of God.

Dr. B. B. Warfield left us with these words and I leave them with you:

> Redeemed by Christ, regenerated by the Holy Spirit, justified through faith, received into the very household of God as his sons, led by the Spirit into the flowering and fruiting activities of the new life, our salvation is still only in process and not yet complete. We still are the prey of temptation; we still fall into sin; we still suffer sickness, sorrow, death itself....When Christ comes... there shall be a new heaven and new earth, in which dwells righteousness.

10. Prayer for Sanctification

For this is the will of God, your sanctification...

1 Thessalonians 4:3

Now I pray to God that you do no evil...

2 Corinthians 13:7

As a pastor the Apostle Paul had the uncomfortable responsibility for the souls of many professing Christians among several particular churches. The Apostle Paul by inspiration from God set the standard for all pastors, commonly known as pastoral theology. Psychology has radically affected the pastoral ministry since many churches focus on the therapeutic model for treating sinful behavior. The therapist sometimes referred to as a psychotherapist helps treat people with mental and emotional problems by talking about the problems. Unfortunately, the therapist has replaced the pastor. That was not the standard set by the Apostle Paul. Using an agricultural metaphor the Bible referred to the church (people of God) as sheep and the pastor (elders) as the shepherd. Paul instructed the elders of the Ephesian Church to shepherd or pastor the church of God. The pastor is a spiritual leader and has the responsibility for the souls of the congregation under his care (Acts 20:28-30). "The elders who are among you I exhort, I who am a fellow elder and a witness of the sufferings of Christ, and also a partaker of the glory that will be revealed: Shepherd the flock of God which is among you, serving as overseers..." (1 Peter 5:1-2).

The Lord expects pastors to feed the flock, not with man-made inventions, but with the Word of God. Pastors must preach, teach and counsel with the whole counsel of God as their authority. The Lord also expects pastors to strengthen the brethren, not with man-made ideas such as managerialism and therapeutic innovations, but with the Word of God.

Programs are not the answer to spiritual growth, which is sanctification. Sunday School, Small Group Meetings, youth programs, weight loss programs and a dozen other programs are not the biblical mandates for the strengthening the souls of men. All these are recent inventions of the liberal church and the shift to a social gospel. A weight loss program may strengthen your body, but it will not strengthen your soul. It is the Spirit of God that enables you to understand God's Word that is the source of your strength.

Paul taught that the pastor has the primary responsibility for equipping the saints for the work of ministry.

> And He Himself gave some to be apostles, some prophets, some evangelists, and some pastors and teachers, for the equipping of the saints for the work of ministry, for the edifying of the body of Christ, till we all come to the unity of the faith and of the knowledge of the Son of God, to a perfect man, to the measure of the stature of the fullness of Christ; that we should no longer be children, tossed to and fro and carried about with every wind of doctrine, by the trickery of men, in the cunning craftiness of deceitful plotting, but, speaking the truth in love, may grow up in all things into Him who is the head—Christ— from whom the whole body, joined and knit together by what every joint supplies, according to the effective working by which every part does its share, causes growth of the body for the edifying of itself in love. (Ephesians 4:11-16)

The standard has been set by the Word of God; however, it does not always mean pastors will be faithful to the Word of God. Sometimes men have falsely perceived that God called them to pastor God's people, when in fact they should be working as a car salesman, a politician, or some other trade in which they can use their silver tongue.

However, some pastors are in their proper place exercising God's gift of preaching, exhortation, teaching, evangelizing, praying, and serving faithfully by example. They are following biblical principles in their quest to equip the saints for the work of ministry.

You would think that doing all the right things would bring pastoral success to the church. That is not so. Next to the Lord Jesus Christ, the Apostle Paul was probably the most gifted pastor in all the Christian church. As a pastor, the Apostle Paul devoted his life to the task of equipping the saints for ministry.

Equipping the saints is directly related to the biblical doctrine of sanctification. The Children's Catechism defines sanctification as "the work of God's free grace, whereby we are renewed in the whole man after the image of God, and are enabled more and more to die unto sin, and live unto righteousness." When your mind and will is renewed, you are then able to put away sin and practice holiness.

The agent of sanctification is the Holy Spirit, but God uses means or instruments in the process of sanctification. The Word of God is the primary means or the primary instrument of our sanctification. It is the pastor's job to explain the Word of God to the congregation, so they will be equipped for works of ministry and therefore grow in their sanctification.

What happens when the pastor does his job, but the congregation doesn't grow in their sanctification? Like Paul prayed, the pastor ought to pray for their sanctification. Paul prayed for the sanctification of the church members in the churches he was acquainted with, because he knew God alone could renew their hearts, minds, wills and affections thus enabling them to grow spiritually. The church at Corinth provides a case study to better understand the application of the doctrine of sanctification. Paul knew that the problems at Corinth were horrible. The problems at Corinth would make any pastor go to his knees in prayer. Paul describes some of the problems at the Corinthian church:

> 1 Corinthians 1:10 - "Now I plead with you, brethren, by the name of our Lord Jesus Christ, that you all speak the same thing and that there be no divisions among you. . . ."

> 1 Corinthians 3:3 - "For where there are envy, strife, and divisions among you, are you not carnal and behaving like mere men?"

> 1 Corinthians 4:18 - "Now some of you are puffed up (arrogant)."

> 1 Corinthians 5:1 - "It is actually reported that there is sexual immorality among you..."

> 1 Corinthians 6:1 - "Dare any of you, having a matter against another, go to law before the unrighteous and now before the saints?"

> 1 Corinthians 6:9-11 - "Do you not know that the unrighteous will not inherit the kingdom of God? Do not be deceived. Neither fornicators, nor idolaters, nor adulterers, nor homosexuals, nor sodomites, nor thieves, nor covetous, nor drunkards, nor revilers, nor extortions will inherit the kingdom of God. And such were some of you. . . ."

> 1 Corinthians 11:18 - "For first of all, when you come together as a church, I hear that there are divisions among you. . . .."

With so many problems in the church you might think the great Apostle would throw up his hands and say "I give up." However, Paul didn't give up. He worked and he prayed. Pastor Paul prayed for their sanctification. Every pastor ought to pray for the sanctification of the congregation.

Paul prayed for the Corinth Church that they "may be made complete" (2 Corinthians 13:9). Paul does not have Christian perfectionism in mind. The word "complete" comes from the Greek word *katartizw*. Jesus used the word referring to those who are "fully trained" (Luke 6:40). When an unskilled worker is trained he is reformed in his thinking and practice. The word was originally used to refer to "putting something in a proper condition."

Paul prays that the Corinthian church will be made complete or we might say the prayer was that they would be reformed in their thinking and practice. The Corinthian church was in need of reformation and restoration. They needed to be reformed by the Word of God. They needed to repair the division, strife, envy, arrogance and immoral behavior that had put their spiritual growth on hold. Their sanctification was in reverse.

Paul's prayer for the congregation at Corinth included a negative command (do not command) and a positive command (do command). First, his prayer is that they would do no evil. This command is necessary for all Christian believers to progress in their sanctification. Second, his prayer is that they should do what it honorable.

The word "honorable" is rarely used this day and age. It derives from the Greek word *kalos*, which refers to the good and the beautiful. When it applies to one's character it takes the form of virtue and excellence.

Paul prayed that they would seek harmony and union rather than separation and division. He wanted them to seek peace and concord rather than strife and disagreement. Paul prayed they would show compassion and benevolence rather than envy and jealousy and they would replace arrogance with humility and decent moral behavior than immoral behavior.

True harmony, peace, benevolence, and humility are marks of spiritual growth. Those are the things that the congregation at Corinth needed to do to repair the broken relationships with each other - with their pastor, the Apostle Paul and ultimately with God Himself.

When we pray for sanctification of the members of the church, we are praying for the reformation of the church. We are praying that its members will be kept from sin, grow in grace, and increase in holiness.

Is your prayer the same as Paul's prayer? If you are praying for the sanctification of the church, then you must be praying for the edification of the church and not the destruction of the church. Edification will come if you will honor the truth from the Word of God. I hope you will pray collectively with the church as the Apostle Paul and his company prayed: "We pray that you may be made complete."

11. Prayer for Wisdom and Revelation

Therefore I also, after I heard of your faith in the Lord Jesus and your love for all the saints, do not cease to give thanks for you, making mention of you in my prayers: that the God of our Lord Jesus Christ, the Father of glory, may give to you the spirit of wisdom and revelation in the knowledge of Him, the eyes of your understanding being enlightened...

Ephesians 1:15-18

The prayers of the Apostle Paul reflect the passion of a pastor's heart. Godly pastors should serve faithfully and watch over the congregation as a shepherd watches over his sheep. He has an interest in their salvation and spiritual growth.

The pastor may plan Bible studies or teach on a special subject for the spiritual well-being of the congregation. However, all the studies and efforts are not enough. The pastor should set the example by praying for the congregation of God's people and teaching for their spiritual growth.

Paul's prayer for the congregation at Ephesus was a prayer for wisdom and revelation. Every pastor ought to pray for God to give every member of the congregation a spirit of wisdom and a spirit of revelation for the spiritual growth of the entire congregation. Paul prayed "that the God of our Lord Jesus Christ, the Father of glory, may give you a spirit of wisdom..." (Ephesians 1:17). Paul's prayer is an example for all pastors to follow.

Many contemporary theologians believe wisdom and ethics are almost synonymous terms. Philosophers categorize wisdom as either theoretical or practical. Christians have the Bible to explain the doctrine of wisdom. Biblical wisdom certainly encompasses ethics, theoretical and practical wisdom, but fundamentally biblical wisdom refers to the way

Christians understand life and how to enjoy God.

Wisdom from a Biblical perspective begins with an awareness of the true and living God. "The fear of the LORD is the beginning of wisdom, and the knowledge of the Holy One is understanding" (Proverbs 9:10). Human consciousness, intelligence and understanding are necessary components of wisdom. There are numerous references to wisdom in the Bible. They are often used along with the rational capacity of man so they are, "filled with wisdom and understanding" (1 Kings 7:14).

Prudence is a mark of wisdom. "I, wisdom, dwell with prudence, and find out knowledge and discretion" (Proverbs 8:12). A prudent person will exercise good judgment and forethought. "The wisdom of the prudent is to understand his way, but the folly of fools is deceit" (Proverbs 14:8). All good things come from God; therefore, wisdom comes from God. The foolish man stands in contrast to the wise man (Ecclesiastes 2:19).

I grant to you that a person who is not a Christian may seem to possess some of these attributes and appear to exercise them, but at the end of his or her life, prudence, discernment, and humility become meaningless. They are of no use at all. The Apostle Paul says it best: "We speak wisdom among those who are mature, yet not the wisdom of this age, nor of the rulers of this age who are coming to nothing." (1 Corinthians 2:6). Natural human wisdom will ultimately lead to condemnation. But wisdom given by the Spirit of God will strengthen your soul.

For Christians, spiritual maturity is a glorious gift, because it is given only to those who have the Holy Spirit as their instructor. For that reason pastors ought to pray that God may give God's people biblical and godly wisdom. It is also the duty of the congregation of God's people to pray for biblical wisdom.

Godly pastors not only pray for wisdom, they pray for the

spirit of revelation. The word "revelation" comes from the Greek word *apokalupsis*. The word "revelation" usually refers to the unveiling of something previously hide. Paul's reference to the "spirit of revelation" must refer to spiritual discernment because the text refers to the revelation of the knowledge of Jesus Christ. It could not be the unveiling of Christ for the first time, because as Christians they already had some knowledge of Christ.

As Christians grow in their sanctification and mature spiritually, the Holy Spirit continually enables them to understand biblical doctrine and put it into practice.

Pastors must be careful to pray for the spirit of wisdom and discernment in the right manner. Christians cannot question the fact that the Holy Spirit is the giver of spiritual life and that He is the enabler for spiritual discernment. Yet they both come through the door of understanding.

God gave Christians a rational mind and the faculty of understanding so that they might learn and know spiritual wisdom. They do not gain spiritual wisdom and spiritual discernment immediately, but rather they gain it mediately. God uses instruments or agents to bring us to understand spiritual wisdom and discernment. The agent for spiritual wisdom and discernment is "the knowledge of Him."

True biblical wisdom is knowing and understanding the nature and character of God and applying that wisdom to life. Discernment without knowledge of God's nature and character is no discernment at all. Spiritual maturity is the result of God's gift namely, the spirit of wisdom and revelation in the knowledge of Him.

Christians gain the knowledge of God by reading the Word of God. They will acquire some knowledge of the triune God by the preaching and teaching of sound doctrine. Read books that teach sound doctrine and discuss your reading with other godly Christians.

The Bible has a warning for those "always learning and

never able to come to the knowledge of the truth" (2 Timothy 3:7). God's warning to the Babylonian ruler: "Your wisdom and your knowledge have warped you and you have said in your heart, I am and there is no one else beside me" (Isaiah 47:10). Paul's warning to the Corinthians: Knowledge puffs up, but love edifies" (1 Corinthians 8:1).

As Christians acquire the knowledge of Jesus Christ, the Spirit of wisdom and discernment will increase for their benefit. The first benefit is the hope of His calling: Salvation secure by God's eternal act of ordination. The second benefit is the glory of His inheritance in the saints: Salvation secure in God's adoption. The third benefit is the exceeding greatness of His power toward His church: Salvation secured by God's all powerful hand.

Paul's prayer for wisdom and revelation is the prayer of all Christians. The doctrine fits the principle of praying for one another. Every professing believer should pray a prayer for wisdom and discernment for other professing believers in the congregation, so they will all reap the benefits of the work of the Holy Spirit.

12. Prayer for Christian Living

For this reason we also, since the day we heard it, do not cease to pray for you, and to ask that you may be filled with the knowledge of His will in all wisdom and spiritual understanding; that you may walk worthy of the Lord, fully pleasing Him, being fruitful in every good work and increasing in the knowledge of God; strengthened with all might, according to His glorious power, for all patience and longsuffering with joy; giving thanks to the Father who has qualified us to be partakers of the inheritance of the saints in the light.

Colossians 1:9-12

Paul prayed for the congregation of God's people at Colossae. It might appear that the prayers of the Apostle Paul are redundant. Paul was not ignorant and he was not at a loss for words. They were pastoral words. Paul's prayer is that the Christians at the Colossian church will be filled with the knowledge of God's will in all wisdom and spiritual understanding.

Paul was concerned for the congregation, for their salvation, for their sanctification, for their spiritual growth, and for their defense and confirmation of the gospel. Paul's prayers are uniquely pastoral. In biblical symbolism the shepherd reminds us of the pastor. Just like the shepherd is responsible for the care of the sheep, the pastor is responsible for the spiritual care of the congregation. Often the shepherd had to stay with the sheep twenty-four hours a day. In the same way a pastor must have the interest of the congregation at heart without a lapse.

Paul had the congregation at heart like a good shepherd because he prayed always for them. He prayed for them because he knew they were weak in their understanding of the doctrine of Christ. For that reason Paul said "We do not cease to pray for you" (Colossians 1:9).

Although Christians should pray for physical and material needs, they should give priority to their spiritual needs. Paul prayed that the Colossians "may be filled with the knowledge of His will in all wisdom and spiritual understanding; that you may walk worthy of the Lord, fully pleasing Him, being fruitful in every good work and increasing in the knowledge of God; strengthened with all might..." (Colossians 1:9-11). Paul did not want anyone to fall into spiritual apostasy. The prayers of the Apostle Paul are primarily and sometimes exclusively for the spiritual needs of the congregation. Spiritual understanding is necessary for sanctification.

Spiritual understanding has to do with who we really are, not who we think we are and who God is not who we think He is. Pray for Christians to be filled with the knowledge of God's will. The prayer is for God to enable Christians to "walk worthy of the Lord." A worthy walk is one that pleases God. So, this prayer is that God will transform the character of the Christian. It is a prayer for Christian living.

The goal in Christian living is to please the Lord. We're nothing but dust and it behooves us to live a God-centered life. A God-centered life is worthy of and pleasing to the Lord. A prayer for a God-centered life is a prayer for Christian living.

Christian living is evident when Christians are "fully pleasing Him" (Colossians 1:10). This is not referring to Christian moral perfection. "Fully pleasing" means to please Christ in every responsibility and duty of Christian life. Christian living also refers to "being fruitful in every good work" (Colossians 1:10). The one who walks worthy of the Lord is busy in the Lord's vineyard. Jesus said, "Every good tree bears good fruit, but a bad tree bears bad fruit" (Matthew 7:17). Here Paul shows us that the Lord is pleased with various kinds of good works. Your good works will never produce salvation, but good works will certainly follow salvation. Practice follows doctrine. Christian living cannot be separated from enlarging our understanding God's nature and character.

Paul's prayer included a request for the congregation that they would be "strengthened with all might, according to His glorious power..." (Colossians 1:11). The source for strength, might, and power is divine. A fruitful ministry and increasing in the knowledge of God is the work of the triune God. The strength Paul mentioned is not merely intellectual strength. It is dangerous to trust the intellect for salvation and spiritual growth. The prayer of a godly pastor who does not cease to pray for the congregation of God's people is instrumental in bringing spiritual strength to the family of God. Spiritual strength only comes from God. It is strength that does not come from our feeble intellectual, psychological or physical strength. It is strength greater than our own strength.

When God called Joshua to work in His kingdom, God told Joshua, "be strong and of good courage" (Joshua 1:9). Joshua would need strength for battle, but more important he would need strength of character to please God. Likewise, you will need strength for Christian living.

Even though the Holy Spirit endows you with spiritual power for Christian living, you will face testing, trials, and temptation. The prayer for strength is a prayer for patience and longsuffering with joy. The Word of God does not hide the reality of suffering. "For to you it has been granted on behalf of Christ, not only to believe in Him, but also to suffer for His sake..." (Philippians 1:29).

13. Prayer for Providential Guidance

For what thanks can we render to God for you, for all the joy with which we rejoice for your sake before our God, night and day praying exceedingly that we may see your face and perfect what is lacking in your faith? Now may our God and Father Himself and our Lord Jesus Christ, direct our way to you. And may the Lord make you increase and abound in love to one another and to all, just as we do to you, so that He may establish your hearts blameless in holiness before our God and Father at the coming of our Lord Jesus Christ with all His saints.

1 Thessalonians 3:9-13

The prayers of the Apostle Paul certainly teach Christians not only about his prayer life, but what our prayer life should be like. From the prayers we've already examined, it is obvious that we should pray for our own salvation and the salvation of others. We know we should pray for spiritual growth.

Prayer is relative to the Spirit of God in the soul of man. Prayer is first directed to God on behalf of our spiritual relationship to God and for the relationships with other people, both Christians and unbelievers.

Too often I hear professing Christians pray for some pressing physical need and make urgent appeals for some physical or psychological need. However, when the crisis is over prayer is not mentioned again until another crisis. It seems as if we think that God is only interested in our immediate pressing needs. God is uniquely concerned about every part of our existence.

God exists apart from creation. God does not depend on anything for His existence. God is not derived from any source. There is no uncertainty with God. If we can grasp an understanding of the nature and character of God from the perspectives I've mentioned in previous chapters, then we know that God is the only possible source of all other existence.

Christians pray to God for specific reasons, but they should remember that He is the source of all creation. Therefore, it is logical that He will sustain, provide for and govern what He creates. Christian theology refers to it as the doctrine of providence. There are many examples of God's providence in the Word of God. One of the most descriptive is found in Genesis chapter twenty-two. It is the account of Abraham taking his only son, Isaac, to the land of Moriah to offer Isaac as a burnt offering.

The story is brief, but profound. Abraham rose early and saddled his donkey. He split the wood for the sacrifice and went to the place designated by God. On his way Isaac asked Abraham, "where is the lamb for the offering?" Abraham answered, "My son, God will provide for Himself the lamb for a burnt offering." (See Genesis chapter twenty-two for the complete story.)

The doctrine of providence is an important dimension of the pastoral ministry. There are four dimensions to the providence of God.

1. Sustenance - God sustains what He creates. Everything in the universe is dependent on the being and power of God.

2. Provision - God not only creates, but he provides for all things based on his foreordination of all things. His ultimate provision is His Son, Jesus Christ, the only Redeemer of the elect.

3. Government - God governs the world by his

absolute authority and power. He has the right and ability to govern all things that come to pass.

4. Concurrence - It literally means "to run together with". Used in connection with the doctrine of God's providence, it is used when describing the primary and secondary causes and that they operate concurrently. God's purpose is brought to pass by his sovereignty even though he uses human means. An example of the doctrine of concurrence is found in Genesis where the brothers of Joseph (Genesis 37-50) did evil, but God meant it for good.

Paul's prayer for the Thessalonians reflects his pastoral understanding of the doctrine of providence. Christians may ask, "Why do we need to pray if God already knows our needs and has already planned for our needs?" The answer is simple. We are creatures and we need to experience our relationship with God. He speaks to us through Scripture and we speak to Him through prayer. Prayer, bending the knee, and bowing reflects humility and a state of dependency. All rational beings, men and angels, are utterly dependent and God is supremely independent. We pray for God's providential care because He is sovereign and we need someone to call on greater than ourselves.

Paul had an interest in the redemption of the saints at Thessalonica. We should learn to pray like Paul prayed. "Now may our God and Father Himself, and our Lord Jesus Christ direct our way to you" (1 Thessalonians 3:11). Paul emphasized the unity of God the Father and God the Son. The unity of the God-head is certainly emphasized here, but Paul also looks away from himself; He looks heavenward. During the reign of Hezekiah in the Old Testament the priests stood to give the benediction and the Bible says they "blessed the people, and their voice was heard; and their prayer came up to

His holy dwelling place, to heaven" (2 Chronicles 30:27).

If we pray rightly, we then step out of ourselves, as it were, when we offer prayers to God in the name of Christ who is in heaven standing on our behalf. Our prayers must be consistent with our relationship with God.

Paul prayed that he and those with him might have a prosperous journey to the Thessalonians. When we decide to take a trip, how often do we pray that God will direct the way? It is in God that we live and move and have our being. We depend on God for every thought and action in this life. When we come to a crisis in life we find ourselves helpless and we turn to God for providential guidance.

Sometimes it is not possible to know the way God would have us go:

> Which school to go to....?
> Which person to marry...?
> Which business endeavor to follow...?
> Where should I live...?
> Thousands of other decisions...?

The Bible teaches us general principles to follow in making many decisions. It may be hard work to dig out those principles, but they are there.

When we pray for God to direct our way, we must never ask Him something against His will. Make sure we are consistent with His known will and pray diligently for God to direct the way.

Prayer must be offered for the prosperity and spiritual growth of the church. "May the Lord make you increase and abound in love to one another and to all...?" (1 Thessalonians 3:12). Here Paul expresses his desire for the church at Thessalonica. However, Paul's desire depends on the providential care from God. Paul didn't have the power to make the church increase and abound in love to one another and to all, but the Lord does have that power. Mutual love is required of all Christians, but Christian love is often misunderstood. In 1 Corinthians 13 Paul says this:

> Love is kind;
> Love rejoices in truth.

Sometimes truth does not have the appearance of kindness. For instance we know the Bible requires us to worship collectively on the Sabbath day. If God's people do not gather, the loving thing to do is to remind them of their duty before God. There may be some reason they cannot attend, therefore you need not remind them, just pray for them. If they are not providentially hindered you will show your love to them by confronting them with their sin. Biblical love is more often associated with rational truth than it is with emotional experiences. In any case, we should pray that God's providence will make our love abound to one another.

Christians pray for God's providential guidance so the Lord may establish their hearts blameless in holiness before our God and Father at the coming of our Lord Jesus Christ with all His saints.

Holiness is absolutely necessary if we are to ever see heaven. We stand blameless in holiness before God because of the absolute righteousness of Jesus Christ applied to our soul. The increase and abundance of love toward one another is evidence of the holiness being perfected in us by the God who saved us from eternal damnation.

I hope you will make it a matter of your own private worship to pray a prayer for God's providential guidance to lead you before His throne in holiness. The Apostle began his prayer with a request that in the providence of God Paul and his company could journey to Thessalonica.

We too are on a journey. Day by day we move closer to

our destination. One day we will arrive and stand before our Lord, our Creator, our Judge, our Savior and our Provider. While you are on that journey please take time to pray and pray regularly for God's providential guidance.

14. Prayer for the Glory of God

Therefore we also pray always for you that our God would count you worthy of this calling, and fulfill all the good pleasure of His goodness and the work of faith with power, that the name of our Lord Jesus Christ may be glorified in you, and you in Him, according to the grace of our God and the Lord Jesus Christ.

2 Thessalonians 1:11-12

The Apostle Paul prayed regularly for the various congregations in Asia Minor and southern Europe. It is worth noting that Paul's Prayers are not first person singular. Paul said, "We pray" which implies that Christians should join in prayer with him and pray for each other. The Apostle Paul enjoins us to pray without ceasing "in order that the name of our Lord Jesus Christ may be glorified in you and you in Him.

The manifestation of God's presence is His glory in you. It is a reflection of His glory in the church. The prayer Paul prayed for the church at Thessalonica should be your prayer privately and collectively for the church. Christians ought to be instructed by Paul's prayer for the glory of God.

Pray that God may count you worthy of your calling. Paul prayed that the church "may be counted worthy of the Kingdom of God" (2 Thessalonians 1:5). Anyone who is worthy of the kingdom of God is worthy only because of the righteousness of Jesus Christ. Without the righteousness of Christ applied to the soul, no one can stand before a righteous God. So our worthiness in the kingdom of God is the result of justification by faith through grace because of Christ. Therefore Christ makes us worthy of our calling.

We must not take for granted that Christ makes us worthy of the kingdom of God. Our worthiness is a privilege and honor given to us by the Lord. The story of the Centurion sending for Jesus to heal his slave brings the concept of worthiness into perspective. When Jesus was approaching the Centurion's house the Centurion said, "Lord do not trouble yourself further, for I am not worthy for you to come under my roof" (Luke 7:6). The Centurion was a man of authority, but a humble man aware that he stood unworthy before the Lord. Christians need to give more attention to their unworthiness. It will remind them of their need to pray that God will count them worthy of their calling.

> Pray that they will be counted worthy of their calling in salvation.

> Pray that they will be counted worthy of their calling in sanctification.

> Pray that they will be counted worthy of their calling in spiritual growth and Christian living.

> Pray that they will be counted worthy of their calling in the defense and confirmation of the gospel.

Paul prayed that God would fulfill all the good pleasure of His goodness and the work of faith with power. I take it that Paul's reference to "goodness" is a reference to the fruit of the Spirit. Goodness is not merely a condition of the Christian soul, it is a necessary condition that expresses itself in good actions "for it is God who works in you both to will and to do for His good pleasure" (Philippians 2:13). Like worthiness we must never forget that if there is any desire for goodness in us, it comes from God. Paul prayed that God may fulfill every desire for goodness. If you have a desire to do the good and right thing in love and humility, then the glory of God shines forth in you.

Lift up your head and humble your heart as you pray for the glory of God to be manifested in you. When Christians pray for each other according to the Word of God, they pray for the glory of God in His church.

When King David charged the congregation of God's people to support Solomon in the building of the Temple David prayed: "Yours O Lord is the greatness, the power and the glory. . ."

We pray: "Thine is the kingdom and the power and the glory forever."

15. Difficult Prayers

This book was born out of my desire to examine the Lord's model prayer. There was so much more to say about the biblical doctrine of prayer, so I decided to summarize Paul's prayer life. The Bible is richly adorned with prayer accompanied by God's blessing. However, prayer is not like a vending machine. Prayer is a means of grace according to the will of God, which I explained in chapter four. I want to summarize the meaning and exercise of prayer.

"Prayer is nothing else than the opening up of our heart before God," so said John Calvin in his commentary on Isaiah. The Lord Himself commands us to pray, but why do we have to be commanded to pray?   God created us, sustains us, governs us, redeemed us and gives us His grace, so it should be natural to offer up our desires to God. The Psalmist says, "Pour out your heart before Him; God is a refuge for us" (Psalm 62:8).   Christians should empty themselves before the Lord so that their desires are presented to the Lord.

It is a great privilege to appear before God with our desires, but because we are sinners we need Christ to intercede for us.   Since we are sinners, we must approach Him humbly with a contrite heart.   The Psalmist left Christians with these words; "I acknowledged my sin to you, and my iniquity I have not hidden. I said 'I will confess my transgression to the Lord,' and you forgave the iniquity of my sin" (Psalm 32:5). Christians will find refuge in God, but they must seek His mercy in humility and confession of sin in prayer.

Prayer must be offered earnestly with thanksgiving (Colossians 4:3). The Word of God instructs us to "pray without ceasing" (1 Thessalonians 5:17). The question is often asked, "How can we pray without ceasing?" This is an action that is habitually repeated at regular intervals with perseverance, but perseverance in prayer is conditioned by a thankful heart. Christians can continue in prayer because of their gratitude for God's providential care and faithfulness to His elect.

Prayer is a means of grace when Christians offer prayer according to the will of God as expressed in his Word. Prayer is the speech of the soul when it is offered in Christ, with confession of sin, and thankful acknowledgment of his mercies. (*Doctrine of Sound Words*, by Martin Murphy, p.393-394)

Theologians refer to the plenary verbal inspiration of Scripture to explain the full authority of each word inspired by God recorded in the Bible. Therefore, Christians believe the full counsel of God and they believe the Bible teaches the nature and character of God. They believe God is a loving God, but He is also a God of justice. Misunderstanding God's nature and character will lead to misunderstanding the doctrine of biblical prayer.

The Book of Psalms provides a guide to prayer life for Christians. Book of Psalms has a wide range of literary form expressed with deep and passionate emotions. There are Psalms of praise and thanksgiving. They recognize God's providential care and answer to prayer. However there are Psalms of lament and imprecatory Psalms.

Imprecatory prayers are justice or judgment Psalms. The concept of justice has not only been abused by many evangelical preachers, justice has been abandoned. God is a just judge. Justice manifests God's love and holiness. Justice does not overlook love, but justice does not abandon holiness. Since justice Psalms are part of Holy Scripture can they be ignored? Some Christians claim these imprecatory Psalms are not for the church today. Others claim that God is love and imprecatory prayers are not for New Testament.

When I was ordained, I made this vow. "Lord, make me a watchman, as the prophets of old, to warn not only myself, but the whole church of the judgments of God and boldly declare the saving grace of Jesus Christ for the salvation of men, women, boys and girls." Christians must not overlook the judgments of God. Imprecatory prayers are made to God and we appeal to God as He alone can exercise His love, righteousness, kindness, and judgment, on earth.

David's prayer in Psalm thirty-one is the inspired Word of God and it serves as a model for our prayers in this wicked age. David prayed with confidence to a sovereign God. "But as for me, I trust in You, O LORD; I say, 'You are my God.' My times are in Your hand. Deliver me from the hand of my enemies, and from those who persecute me" (Psalm 31:14-15). Prayer with confidence begins with belief. The Psalmist doesn't seem to be shy, ashamed or disillusioned to pray with a sense of confidence. David understood God is sovereign. When Christians pray, they must believe the Lord is sovereign and thus have complete confidence in the sovereign Lord.

Although David faced adversaries and was greatly afflicted, he prayed to God for a blessing. His prayer was simple. "Make your face shine upon Your servant" (Psalm 31:16). His entreaty to God was passionate. It was a prayer asking for physical and spiritual well-being. He prayed for the special presence of God.

Some Bible scholars classify Psalm thirty-one as an individual lament. However, there are elements of imprecation. Psalm thirty-one is a prayer to vindicate the righteousness of God. The Psalmist identifies the wickedness raising its ugly head against the righteous.

> Do not let me be ashamed, O LORD, for I have called upon You; Let the wicked be ashamed; Let them be silent in the grave. Let the lying lips be put to silence, which speak insolent things proudly and contemptuously against the righteous. (Psalm 31:17-18)

Pray to your sovereign God when you are confronted by the wicked enemies of God. Charles Spurgeon commented on this Psalm.

> God's people may well look with derision upon their enemies since they are the objects of divine contempt. They scoff at us, but we may with far greater reason laugh them to scorn, because the Lord our God considers them as less than nothing and vanity.

This is the essence of an imprecatory Psalm. It is a prayer for justice, but not with a sense of hatred and bitterness. It is a prayer to honor the character and essence of God. We hear the words "Let the wicked be ashamed" and think that it is an isolated reference.

> Psalm 35:26 – "Let them be ashamed and brought to mutual confusion who rejoice at my hurt."

> Psalm 40:14 – "Let them be ashamed and brought to mutual confusion who seeks to destroy my life."

> Psalm 70:2 – "Let them be ashamed and confounded who seek my life."

> Psalm 97:7 – "Let them be put to shame who serve carved images, who boast of idols."

Jeremiah 17:18 – "Let them be ashamed who persecute me and do not let me be put to shame."

Are you thinking to yourself, "How can I pray like this?" The summary to the answer is, "There is no evidence that this portion of God's Word is abrogated." This is not a personal vindictive prayer. These prayers appeal to the righteousness of God. The Psalmist sees the goodness of God in God's justice. The Psalmist does not try to hide God's holiness. The Psalmist prays that God will be vindicated of any false accusations. Christians ought to pray for victory over the enemy of truth and righteousness.

Psalm thirty-five is classified as an imprecatory prayer. David prays for the righteous judgment of God to prevail. We see a display of his vigor and enthusiasm working through his whole being, especially his emotional tensions. The text of Psalm thirty-five reveals certain characteristics that will help us understand how to pray this Imprecatory Psalm.

David calls on the Lord to act in his behalf against the enemies of God. David expresses in words the feelings of our hearts when injustice surrounds us and overtakes us. David wants to see the justice of God fall on the head of the enemy. David prays for God's presence during this time of persecution. He prays to God: "Vindicate me, O Lord my God, according to Your righteousness..." (Psalm 35:24).

Those unnamed men in this Psalm who are seeking to destroy David are ungodly men. Ungodly men are enemies of God. I remember reading a comment by John Calvin on this and although I do not remember the exact quote, let me paraphrase. "When the ungodly gird and prepare themselves for destroying the Church, they are usually inflated with intolerable pride." Pride is the root sin and David is praying that the identifying marks will bring them to repentance. The goal of this prayer is not destruction, but repentance.

The Psalmist prays for several specific things to happen to

the impenitent sinner. First, he prayed that they would be ashamed. (Psalm 35:26). Let the sinner see himself for what he is. Pray that the outward appearance will correspond with inward character of the enemy of God, so it will bring him to repentance. Second, he prayed for the impenitent sinner to have a loss of dignity. Literally David prayed for the enemies of God to be humiliated" (Psalm 35:26). Humility of the proud leads to disgrace, confusion, and embarrassment. The prayer calls for forced humiliation, because humility is the antidote for pride.

There is hope in the redemption of God's people. "Let them shout for joy and be glad, who favor my righteous cause" (Psalm 35:27). The reason for vindication is for the purpose of giving glory to a righteous God. The fundamental idea is that the righteousness of God will manifest itself by the salvation that comes from God. The Psalmist prays with hope for God's justice which will result in the redemption of God's people. A godly man is marked by his hope of redemption from a just God.

The hinge upon which imprecatory prayers turn is the glory of God. "And let them say continually, The Lord be magnified" (Psalm 35:27). Imprecatory prayers belong to the Lord; Not me; Not you!

Imprecatory prayers signify the righteousness of God. Therefore, pray for the salvation of the enemies of God. Your tongue is to praise God for His righteousness and your expectation of the eternal inheritance of his righteousness.

The justice of a just God will have its effect on ungodly people one way and godly people in another way. We are reminded of the words of the Apostle Paul to the Corinthian Church. The gospel is the aroma of death to some and the aroma of life to others (2 Corinthians 2:15-16).

Are imprecatory prayers difficult to you? They probably are. I know they are for me. However, imprecatory prayers remain a part of God's infallible word and we must believe

God gave them for His glory. If our confidence and commitment is in order, then we must pray to a sovereign God when confronted by the wicked men of this world.

Someone may be thinking, "But Jesus said love your enemies and pray for those who persecute you." Jesus also said, "Woe to you scribes and Pharisees, hypocrites! For you shut up the kingdom of heaven against men; for you neither go in yourselves, nor do you allow those who are entering to go in" (Matthew 23:13).

So how must you respond to these imprecations? You must respond positively. Pray according to the biblical doctrine, not according to your own personal emotional and vindictive whim. Imprecatory prayers are not hasty emotional expressions applicable to the people of the Old Testament. Pray these prayers as if though Christ Himself were praying them, because ultimately if they are heard in the heavenly courts, they must be mediated by Christ Himself.

16. Practical Prayer

Christians should think about what they say as they pray. Below are a few suggestions to remember when you talk to the King of the universe and Lord of your life.

"Be Anxious for nothing, but in everything by prayer and supplication with thanksgiving let your requests be made known to God" (Philippians 4:6).

O Lord God, eternal, almighty, creator of heaven and earth, and giver of life, we bow before you and pour forth our prayers in the name of Jesus Christ.

Pray for the unconverted in every professing church, especially the ones who "have a form of godliness but deny its power." And that the Spirit of God will renew their spirit and mind...giving them the desire to hear the law and the gospel.

Pray for the shepherds (pastors and preachers) who have abandoned theology and replaced it with their own feelings. Pray that God will convict them of their sins and guide them to return to the old ways.

Pray believing the promise that Christ our Mediator will intercede for us.

Our Father in heaven, we hallow your great and majestic name. We know that your name is the perfection of holiness and dignity.

We pray, O Father in heaven, that your kingdom will come with authority over us and with power to govern us.

We pray that your will be done as your children submit in true obedience to your will.

O Lord if it pleases you to supply all our needs we are forever thankful for your goodness and mercy.

In our time of temptation, we pray You will not allow us to fall under the weakness of our flesh.

When our enemies attack us strengthen us in the Holy Spirit and equip us for the spiritual work to which you have called us.

We examine ourselves and confess that we are unworthy of your generous saving grace.

We pray for the propagation of the gospel and the kingdom of Christ to all nations, for salvation of the Jews, the Muslims, and all ungodly religions. We pray that the Lord will be pleased to bring the entire Islamic world to faith, repentance and conversion.

Help us understand the mysteries of salvation and eternal life, which require spiritual discernment.

Furnish the elders of the church will wisdom and clarity of speech to rightly divide the Word of God, to every person who will hear the Word for the salvation of the soul.

Give thanks for the gracious hand of our Lord as He provides our daily bread and especially for the spiritual bread we receive each Lord's Day.

Pray that God will bring His people into the ministry of the church for the building up of the saints of God for the work of service.

Pray that God the Holy Spirit will convict the hearts of His people to oppose idolatry, murder, gossip, slander, or any other sin that brings shame and grief to the church.

Pray that God will continue to bring His people together for worship, for His glory and for His kingdom. . . .And that He will preclude those who try to bring idolatry and false worship into the church.

Pray that people will turn to God with true discernment, and to abide in Him through living faith; that, finding now the comfort of His presence, they may also have full confidence and assurance in the Lord Jesus Christ for all that is to come.

Pray for the President of the United States, for the Senate and Congress, for all officers and those enlisted in the defense of our country, upon land, and on the water, and in the air.

Pray that God will direct and prosper all their consultations to the advancement of His glory, the good of His Church, the safety, honor and welfare of His people; That all things may be so ordered and settled by their endeavors, upon the best and surest foundations, that peace, happiness, truth and justice will prevail so that true religion may be established among us for all generations.

Give thanks for the Lord's mercies throughout another week, in the blessing of Christian homes and families, daily work, good health, preservation from accident, and hidden dangers....And the blessing of covenant children as they respond to Christian teaching and example both at home and in the congregation's worship.

Pray that the Lord may be pleased to pour out His Spirit, sending upon His church those "seasons of refreshing from the presence of the Lord" which are spoken of in the book of Acts....And first moving His people to pray and confess their sins, owning their entire inadequacy without His power and help.

Pray for the spread of the gospel on a world wide scale, but never forgetting that our personal witness is required as a testimony of God's grace in our lives.

Pray for the many Christians throughout the world who are in prison for their faith in Christ....And for others who are persecuted or who have been banished from their homes and livelihoods as a result of confessing faith in Christ.

Pray for the preaching ministry and that hearts will be warmed and souls will be set ablaze with a zeal that will be contagious to family and friends. Pray for the sick and afflicted among us....And those who cannot attend worship....And others who are not attending worship.

About the Author

Martin Murphy has a B.A. in Bible from Columbia International University and Master of Divinity from Reformed Theological Seminary. Martin spent nearly thirty years in the class room, the pulpit, the lectern, the study, and the library. He now devotes most of his time consolidating academic and practical gains by writing books. He and his wife Mary live in Dothan, Alabama. He is the author of twelve Christian books.

The Church: First Thirty Years, 344 pages, ISBN 9780985618179, $15.95. This book is an exposition of the Book of Acts. It will help Christians understand the purpose, mission, and ministry of the church.

The Dominant Culture: Living in the Promised Land, 172 pages, ISBN 970991481118, $11.95. This book examines the culture of Israel during the period of the Judges. It explains how worldviews influence the church and it reveals biblical principles to help Christians learn how to live in the culture.

My Christian Apology, 98 pages, ISBN 9780984570874, $7.95. This book investigates the doctrine of Christian apologetics. It explains rational Christian apologetics.

The Essence of Christian Doctrine, 200 pages, ISBN 9780984570812, $12.95. This book was written so that pastors and laymen would have a quick reference to major biblical doctrines. Dr. Steve Brown says it was written, "with clarity and power about the verities of the Christian faith and in a way that makes a difference in how we live."

Return to the Lord, 130 pages, ISBN 9780984570805, $8.95. This book is an exposition of Hosea. The prophet speaks a message of repentance and hope. Hosea's prophetic message to Old Testament and New Testament congregations is, "you have broken God's covenant; return to the Lord." Dr. Richard Pratt said, "We need more correct and practical instruction in the prophetic books, and you have given us just that."

Theological Terms in Layman Language, 130 pages, ISBN 9780985618155, $8.95. This book was written so that simple words like faith or not so simple words like aseity are explained in plain language. Theological Terms in Layman Language is easy to read and designed for people who want a brief definition for theological terms. The terms are in layman friendly language.

Brief Study of the Ten Commandments, 164 pages, 9780991481163, $10.95. This book will help Christians discover or re-discover the meaning of the Ten Commandments.

The Present Truth, 164 pages, ISBN 9780983244172, $8.95. Each chapter examines a topic relative to the Christian life. Topics such as church, sin, anger, marriage, education and more.

Doctrine of Sound Words: Summary of Christian Theology, 423 pages, ISBN 9780991481125, $16.95. This is a book of Christian doctrine in topical format. It covers a wide range of theological topics such as, the triune God, creation, providence, sin, justification, repentance, Christian liberty, free will, marriage and divorce, Christian fellowship, et al). There are thirty three topics beginning with "Holy Scriptures" and ending with "The Last Judgment." It is a systematic theology for laymen based on the full counsel of God.

Friendship: The Joy of Relationships, ISBN 9780986405518, 48 pages, $6.49. This is the kind of book that friends give each other and share the principles with each other. If friends do not feel comfortable sharing these relationship principles with each other, the friendship may not really exist. Friendship involves a relationship of distinction. It is a relationship that respects the dignity of another person. The Bible teaches a different version of what it means to be a friend than the popular culture teaches. There are many occasions when friends say they are friends, but they are not friends. "Even my own familiar friend in whom I trusted, who ate my bread, has lifted up his heel against me" (Psalm 41:9). A true friend will endure and sacrifice for a friend. "A friend loves at all times" (Proverbs 17:7) and "there is a friend who sticks closer than a brother" (Proverbs 18:24).

Ultimate Authority for the Soul, ISBN 9780986405501, 151 pages, $9.99. What is the ultimate authority for human beings? This book examines that question and concludes that every rational being has some recognition of God as the ultimate authority. Although God is the ultimate authority, He confers His authority by means of the Word of God. The author examines Psalm 119 to build a defense for the ultimate authority for the soul. Although this book was written for Christians, the author builds the case that authority is a principle necessary to maintain sanity and order in the family, the church and civil society. The Word of God connects the soul with reality.

www.ingramcontent.com/pod-product-compliance
Lightning Source LLC
Chambersburg PA
CBHW061754020426
42331CB00006B/1470